AF372138

Training the Alsatian
(German Shepherd Dog)

Training
the Alsatian

(German Shepherd Dog)

The Obedient Companion
or Working Partner

John Cree

PELHAM BOOKS
London

First published in Great Britain by
Pelham Books Ltd
52 Bedford Square,
London, WC1B 3EF
1977

© John Cree, 1977

All Rights Reserved. No part of this publication
may be recorded, stored in a retrieval system,
or transmitted, in any form or by any means,
electronic, mechanical, photocopying, recording
or otherwise, without the prior permission
of the Copyright owner.

ISBN 0 7207 0993 8

Phototypeset by Saildean Limited
Printed in Great Britain by
Billing & Sons Ltd,
Guildford, London and Worcester

TO IRENE MY WIFE

She has looked after our two daughters, our dogs and myself. She has encouraged, sympathised and criticised. She has typed and retyped the manuscript. Without her help there could not have been a book.

Contents

Illustrations (between pages 96 and 97)

Line Drawings

Acknowledgements

The writing of a book can never be the complete work of one person. The author may sit down and put pen to paper, but the knowledge expressed is invariably an accumulation from many sources. I am no exception, and a special acknowledgement is due to the seasoned competitors and trainers who instructed and encouraged me during my early years of dog training. Names that come readily to mind are Jim Whytock and Jack Grant from my home club in Dundee, also Jean Faulks from Aberdeen and Jack Todd from Edinburgh. Although the writing of this book would not have been possible without the foundation gained during these early years, the production of the manuscript, line drawings, photographs and appendices have been made practical through the help and encouragement of many others.

Advice on presentation was gratefully received from Joyce Stranger, with Jean Faulks, Fiona McFadyen and my daughter Joyce Rae helping to examine the manuscript for improvements. The line drawings were carefully prepared by Evelyn McKenna and most of the photographs supplied by Mike McFadyen and my son-in-law, Colin Ball. The appendices were mainly the responsibility of Fiona McFadyen, who obtained a great deal of the information from *Kennel Club Stud Books* borrowed from the Scottish Kennel Club, Mrs M. Lindsay Smith and details supplied by Vivian Kershaw of *Dog Training Weekly*, with the names of the various police dog handlers being obtained from Inspector 'Timber' Wood.

I must make a special 'thank you' to Carine Fairbairn and Rob Patterson for their struggle through heavy snow to borrow the *Stud Books* from Mrs Lindsay Smith.

My appreciation goes out to all who helped to make this book possible.

Abbreviations

C.C.	Chief Constable
C.D.	Companion Dog
Ch.	Champion
Ex.	Excellent
G.S.D.	German Shepherd Dog
Int.	International
Ob.	Obedience
P.D.	Police Dog
Sch. H.I, II, III	Schutzhund (Guard or Defence Dog)
T.D.	Tracker Dog
U.D.	Utility Dog
Unr.	Unregistered
v.d.	von der (of the)
W.D.	Working Dog
W.T.	Working Trials

Introduction

This book is written primarily for the Alsatian owner, whether he is responsible for one dog or a breeder with a large kennel. Anyone owning an Alsatian should know how to educate himself and his dog to ensure the fullness of their companionship. He should also know something of his dog's potential and the training which can be carried out to change that companionship into a partnership. The possibilities of this breed are commonly known from police, security and mountain rescue work, and from their contribution as guide dogs, but those are all specialised jobs calling for specialised conditions of work.

Most Alsatians settle into private homes, with the main outlet for the development of their intelligence and character restricted to training for working trials and obedience competitions. However, with a basic knowledge, many pet owners would welcome the chance of developing this intelligence and character to achieve greater satisfaction and companionship.

Control problems can be a worry to many pet dog owners. A dog who will not obey simple requests, will not come when called or will not mix with his owner's friends certainly needs some help. This help can be at hand for an owner ready to learn and apply the basic principles of dog training, and I have tried throughout this book to show one approach to training which has been very successful and should assist pet owners and training enthusiasts alike.

As my own experience is through competing, stewarding and judging at working trials and obedience shows, I have been able to watch the development of characters through the various stages of training. I have also competed and stewarded in the show ring, and have kept close contact with the 'breed'. I am not sure whether my greatest pleasure is taking a dog with working titles into the show ring or going after these working titles with a show winner. It does not really matter, because I believe that they both require each other and the more breeders and working dog owners understand each other's requirements the better the breed will fare.

As for the companion dog owner, what better than understanding the needs of this intelligent breed and doing what he can to develop the character of his companion? After all, dogs that work are first and foremost companions who, through their working ability, have become full partners. The highest reward any owner can have is to feel that his dog has become a full partner through a working relationship.

Our breed is full of character. Let us develop this to the full potential of his inheritance. By training his active mind we shall have a friend who will be grateful for the opportunity to show his value and loyalty.

All Alsatian owners can benefit from dog training. In fact, it is important for the companion dog owner to understand the intelligence of his animal if for no other reason than that he wants to prevent trouble. We all know the name that bad, ignorant or inconsiderate owners have given the breed in the past. The companion dog owner should at least know the basic principles of training and practise them. Preventative training is always much more successful and satisfying than corrective training.

Breeders are not fully equipped for selling puppies unless they understand the problems their stock can create by going into a home which does not appreciate the intelligence that will develop in those little eight-week-old bundles of fur that leave their kennels. I hope the breeders who read this book feel it has been worth their time and that they will encourage new owners to give their new charge an opportunity to develop into an obedient companion or working partner.

Chapter One

What Value in Training?

Why Train?

Any Alsatian owner will find that thoughtful training will develop the character and loyalty of his dog. The wider the breadth of training, the greater the bond between dog and owner. Even the companion dog owner, who just wants an obedient dog, may well find it difficult to resist going a little further and finally deciding to train for competitions. After all, at least ninety-five per cent of today's competitors started with a companion dog and just wanted a well-behaved canine friend. It may also be surprising to find how many of today's 'big names' attended their first training class because they thought they had a problem dog, *only to find that the dog had a problem owner.*

Although my own start was not with a problem dog, it was through a friend who suggested that I would enjoy the local training classes. My first dog was a Labrador puppy and, although we lost him as a puppy, the few months we attended these outdoor classes were sufficient for me to realise that a whole new field of enjoyment had opened up. As you will probably have guessed, my new puppy was an Alsatian, a grand all-rounder who became W.T. Ch. Quest of Ardfern C.D.Ex., U.D. Ex. P.D.Ex. T.D. Ex.

However, the individual or breeder who has no intention of competing in working trials or obedience will find that training for the fun of it will be greatly appreciated by his canine friend.

The Companion Dog

Your puppy may well have been brought into your life as a companion for yourself, your wife or the children. The real joy of this companionship can only become a reality if he behaves and 'does as he is told'. Every day we can see examples of various breeds, including our own, that just do as they please and give dog owners the name of being inconsiderate.

Bringing up a puppy to maturity can be the same as bringing up a child: the mistakes in early life can be difficult to eradicate because when it is discovered that we have lost control he will have probably developed a mind of his own. Any dog will find our weakness long before we find his, and it takes a lot of thinking on our part to reverse this situation. I often wonder if we are completely successful.

To make our companion a fully acceptable member of the community he has to be controllable in the same way as a well-behaved child. We should not have to shout at him or keep pulling on his lead. We are fortunate that our breed accepts gentle discipline; if he becomes a nuisance it is because we have not applied the correct measure of control.

As a companion he requires exercise in both body and mind. It is one thing to give him physical exercise but quite another to keep his mind active in the right direction. The training details that will follow are geared mainly towards the competitive dog, but the companion dog owner will find that the basic approach is the same. The basic training approach is very relevant, with the foundation obedience exercises just as valuable to your companion as the precision exercise is to the competition dog.

The Obedience Partner

The obedience dog is just a companion dog evolved into a sharper thinking and reacting canine friend. Obedience training for competition work adds greatly to the character so long as an overbearing and demanding approach is not applied. One of the dangers of competition obedience training is the obsession with winning at all costs. Unfortunately there are handlers who seem to have forgotten that their dogs are supposed to be companions. These handlers are few and far between but obedience could well do without them. With the correct mental approach to training, both handler and dog will enjoy competing and they will also have their share of winning.

Obedience competitions start with the Beginners class and work through a total of five grades to the top Class C. As would be expected the work becomes progressively more demanding through each stage. The basic grounding, however, can briefly be given as four main exercises:

1   Heel work (on and off lead).
2   Recall to handler.
3   Retrieve an article.
4   Stay while handler moves a distance from the dog.

Any owner who achieves a good mark in each of these exercises with all the distractions of a show will be proud and ready to advance through the more demanding stages of work.

The Working Trials Partner

The trials dog is called upon to display by far the greatest sense of independence whilst working. There are times when he becomes the 'senior' partner in the company, where your training has taught him to become the 'pack leader'. At the same time he must be prepared to accept responsible authority as it is required. He should be able to 'read' your next move and be ready to act in response to your requests.

Very briefly, working trials require the basic teachings for obedience work plus the ability to search and track. Agility tests are also essential, and 'criminal' work can be considered as optional if one wishes to develop in the police dog field of work.

There are four different grades in working trials, from the C.D. (Companion Dog) Stake where obedience, agility and an elementary search cover the work requirements to the top T.D. (Tracker Dog) or P.D. (Police Dog) Stages where a very high degree of nosework or criminal work ability is required.

I have purposely left criminal work out of this book. It is a specialised subject which requires the use of experienced helpers to play the part of 'criminals' and expert tuition on handling. It is a subject I believe should only be passed on through the experience of a good 'criminal' and any written matter should be in instruction manuals intended for reading within the professional bodies who require this knowledge.

The Fully Competitive Partner

I have often heard it said that you cannot mix working trials with obedience or obedience with breed showing. The correct approach to training with the right dog can give you success in each form of competition. It takes a lot of hard work and time to compete in two of these fields and real dedication to be successful in all three.

There has never to date been a triple champion, although there have been a few (very few) champions in breed and obedience or trials and obedience. Only once have we had a breed-trials champion, and this goes back to 1932 when Ch. Benign of Picardy P.D. Ex., U.D. Ex., C.D. Ex., became a working trials champion.

Many people think that the training for obedience adversely affects a working trials dog and vice versa. From my own experience this only happens if the handler is not capable of differentiating between the approaches for both forms of

20

competition. It certainly requires harder work and more thought on the part of the handler, but it can be successfully achieved, and with a happy dog.

The main concern seems to be the mixing of scent discrimination in obedience and searching in working trials. I can only say that within a space of three consecutive Saturdays I worked at two obedience shows and a championship working trial with the following results:

Championship Trials	P.D. Stake: First (which includes a half-mile track and search for judge's articles with steward's scent).
Championship Obedience	Class A: Third (scent discrimination of owner's article). (No Class B at this show). Class C: Third (scent discrimination of judge's scent).
Open Obedience	Class A: First (scent discrimination of owner's article). Class B: First (scent discrimination of judge's article, handler's scent). Class C: Third (scent discrimination of judge's scent).

It will be seen that every nosework exercise was carried out successfully in that short period of time by one dog, my own Quest of Ardfern.

Where to Train

Although this book is prepared in a manner that should give you most of the information you require to achieve a good obedient friend or a working partner, there is no doubt that properly organised training classes are invaluable. You can learn from other people's mistakes, get direct advice on immediate problems, and have your dog accustomed to distractions and other dogs. There is also the social pleasure of meeting and talking with other people who have a common interest.

Training the Alsatian

Although classes can be invaluable, most of the training must be carried out elsewhere, in the house, the garden or a nice quiet piece of ground, and eventually in a park where there are greater distractions. Beginners training should only take about ten to fifteen minutes most days; a day missed now and again does not really matter but a regular daily stint can never be replaced by a hard two-hour session at the weekend.

Some dog owners attend training classes purely to improve their own approach to training, but most take their dogs along because they have a specific problem. A number of these problems can only be solved in the environment in which they occur, but the basic principles and training can be given at organised training sessions. All dog owners wishing to start at these sessions should, however, inform the trainer of any special problems or peculiarities, so that the trainer can take them into consideration during the training session and also give advice on correcting them at home.

There are training clubs in most areas, the majority of them catering for all breeds – there are not many that confine their activities only to Alsatians. Most clubs cater for the pet owner and dogs can graduate from basic training for normal home requirements into the competitive obedience field of work. Help in training for working trials can be obtained through the various working trials societies. Although training sessions are organised for trials work, the handler has to do much more on his own or with individual trials enthusiasts. A number of people do, however, combine both obedience classes and trials training: they attend regular obedience training classes to obtain the advantages of a weekly training session and also train on their own, or with a few friends, to achieve a good working trials standard. Details of the nearest training club or working trials society can be obtained on request from the Kennel Club.

The elementary work at a training club usually covers the exercises required for the Kennel Club beginners routine.

When attending training sessions and listening to all the

advice being given by trainers and other handlers care must be taken to analyse all that has been said. There are many different ways of training a dog and there are many different dogs with different strengths of character. Your approach must be tailor-made to suit your dog. The principles that follow in this book and also the approaches to the different exercises may well require to be modified or moulded to suit your dog. It may also be essential for you to look deeply into your own personality to make it compatible with your present dog if this is necessary.

Competitions

Most obedience clubs do run progress tests and small competitions within their own organisations, although this varies quite a bit from club to club. However, there are open and championship shows throughout the country during most of the year. These shows are held on a Saturday, but midweek shows can be found during the summer months. The number of shows available to you throughout the year depends largely on where you live, also on the time you have available and the cash you are prepared to allocate to this form of pastime.

Working trials societies generally run tracking rallies as well as open and championship trials. Open working trials are normally two-day events, although you can usually carry out your work in one day. Championship trials may run for three or four days, or you may be able to complete all your work in one day, but it is more usual to carry out the tracking and searching on one of the days with all competitors doing the remainder of the work on the final day. The one exception is the C. D. (Companion Dog) Stake, where competitors usually do all their work on the final day.

Full details of the Kennel Club regulations for obedience competitions and working trials are given later in this book. If you are interested in competing they are well worth studying.

Chapter Two

The Alsatian at Home

You, the Owner

Before thinking of buying an Alsatian puppy a prospective owner should take a close look at himself, be honest and ask himself if he is temperamentally suited to look after an animal who is going to be so dependent on him. If you have not owned a dog before you may wonder if you have the knowledge, ability and patience to educate an Alsatian. This knowledge can be gained by reading, asking and observing, but ability depends on the value you place on the knowledge obtained and also the use you make of it. Patience may have to be worked upon, but the keynote to patience is understanding a situation. Educating a dog means gaining control of him through your own self-control.

We normally find that beginners come along to the training club without any knowledge of dog training and usually are very unsure of themselves. It is surprising, however, what hidden talents come to the fore: within six to eight weeks most of these owners have achieved a fair measure of confidence because they can see the progress their dogs have made. Many also find that they possess a greater degree of patience and adaptability than they expected. It is usually the brash 'know-it-all' type who comes unstuck and will drift out because he is not prepared to learn and modify his approach to suit the dog's requirements.

The owner must be prepared to continually look at his own approach – if the dog fails to understand what seems to be a simple request then he should not be too readily blamed. In most cases it is the owner's fault and not the dog's, and insufficient grounding, lack of consistency or an unusual situation can be causes of a dog's failure to understand.

I would like take a simple example of a dog who will not come back when called and look at the possible causes:

insufficient grounding – if, in the past, the dog has been permitted to come back when he wanted to, the ground work has not been prepared for an instant response;

lack of consistency – if the same approach or phraseology is not maintained in calling the dog back, he may not understand his owner's requirements;

an unusual situation – there may be a distraction too great for the measure of control being applied. The distraction of another dog in the vicinity may be beyond the control an owner has over his dog.

It is usually the dog who gets the blame for failing to come when called, but to an expert watching the result may have been a foregone conclusion.

There were two particular instances I remember when I was a very novice handler and was training my first dog, Quest, for working trials. The first was the 'seek back' exercise, which entailed walking through a field with the dog by your side, dropping an article without the dog noticing and walking on for about a hundred yards, then sending the dog back to find the article. My instruction to go back for the article was in the form of an excited question: 'Where is it?' and Quest knew exactly what was wanted. For no apparent reason Quest now seemed to lose the understanding of my requirements, until I realised I had changed my approach from a question to a command: 'Fetch it.' The dog failed to understand the change, and it would have been easy to blame him. This failure on my part indicated how much of a novice I was, but at the same time I was learning through self-analysis.

The other example was during the same period, when we were coming up to a U.D. standard of tracking (tracks half an hour old). Instead of taking the dog on the track in the same direction as the track-layer, I sometimes approached the track at a right angle so that he would have to sort out the correct direction. On some occasions he would start to backtrack, which was very puzzling until I realised he only did this when I laid the track. It was then obvious that, at this stage, he thought he should backtrack on my scent, as my scent was used for the Seek Back. After that I never put him on my tracks at more than a slight angle but varied the approach when someone else laid the track. Quest never backtracked in competition. This only indicates the care that must be taken before blaming the dog for any error or lack of understanding.

Whether it be the owner with a pet dog out on the street or a competition dog doing his best for a handler, it is continually found that dogs are being blamed for some mistake, inattention or downright disobedience when it is apparent that the owner or handler is at fault. We generally find in competition that handlers lose far more marks than the dog, either by their own handling or by their lack of correct training and preparation prior to the show.

The greatest problem with canine education is that of educating the owner (handler). As many people are starting with their first Alsatian and probably their first dog, they learn the hard way with a young puppy who has had no form of behaviour education or an older dog with bad habits. There is no real alternative for the first-time owner but to learn with his dog. Others may help and guide, certainly, but the person or family living with the dog are the only people on the spot to carry out the educational process of teaching an Alsatian to become a social asset and not a liability.

Your Dog

You may be planning to buy a puppy, you may have just taken a young puppy into your home, or you may have taken in a dog who is past the puppy stage. However you acquired him, you must assess the mental and physical suitability of the dog in your home, and again assess them honestly. Most Alsatians are ideal material for training, and in general they are a breed which is willing to please the owner. Temperament, however, does vary considerably and an early assessment can help to determine the approach to be adopted during the early educational process and also the possible limitations to your expectancy of the final result. Physical limitations are probably less obvious but equally important, especially if you wish to develop into the competitive field of working trials.

Character and temperament change as a dog becomes educated, and the quiet timid dog will improve if brought out in the correct manner, which means being introduced to kindly and understanding strangers, mixing with other dogs and most important, getting something to think about. The aggressive dog is probably the result of an incorrect upbringing and may well require some hard and firm handling to make him accept a civilised way of life. Creating an active mind and a real keenness to work can help to put 'nerves' into the background. Although this is not always the case, there is generally a right home for the right dog. If your home is not suited to your dog then I believe your first responsibility is to modify your way of life and help change your dog's approach to life so that you become compatible. It is your responsibility, as the owner, to make every effort possible to let your dog enjoy fully the normal existence of an Alsatian.

If an Alsatian is worth keeping, he is worth training. Even an education in social behaviour helps him become a well-behaved companion. Most Alsatians are worthy and capable of being trained for obedience shows and for working trials, with one exception – police work. This calls for the highest qualities in character and temperament. A shy dog is useless and an uncontrollably aggressive dog worse than useless – an Alsatian should be safe and reliable. Bitches suitable for police work are much more difficult to find than dogs, because with their motherly instincts they can become too protective and unreliable once they have been introduced to this work. We very rarely see a good reliable Alsatian bitch doing police work at working trials. Bitches can, however, excel at tracking and are often unbeatable in the right hands at obedience work. Unfortunately many handlers do not appreciate that bitches can go through a 'broody' period after their season – when this happens it usually becomes noticeable about two or three weeks after the end of the season and normally finishes at the time they would have whelped had they been mated. This condition is not generally noticed in a bitch unless she is being trained for obedience or working trials.

My own bitch Jeza was a prime example of this condition. She was about five weeks out of season when she went for a U.D. championship qualification. About two or three weeks before this I could see this broodiness coming on but I carried on and worked her, and was ashamed of our performance. She had great difficulty in tracking out the first leg. We then tried the search, and if anything this was worse: she had no interest, and no amount of encouragement or help would induce her to work. I apologised to the judge for taking up his time and drove 350 miles home. Just nine weeks after she would have been mated we had the A.S.P.A.D.S. Scottish Championship Trials. Jeza was entered to give support to the event, and because we saw a change in her outlook on life I decided to have a try. She worked a most beautiful fifteen-leg complicated track and then worked her heart out in the search. She did not get enough search articles to qualify but I went home the happiest of failures that day.

This broodiness may not be evident in the companion dog and it often goes unnoticed in the obedience dog, but where a great deal of concentration is required in working trials the problem can become very evident.

There is no such problem with the male species of our breed but the working of a kennel stud dog can have problems. They may tend to be a little bit jealous when bitches are around and although I have not had any problems I have been concerned that a fight could develop at the stay exercises with dogs and bitches mixed. As this is not a major issue at trials and I have never witnessed a fight of this nature it may well indicate that stud dogs will contain their instincts, if properly trained, while their handlers leave them in line at the sit or down stay exercises.

Physical fitness is very important in working trials. Training for the agility tests will soon highlight a dog who is not fit, and hip dysplasia is of major concern to triallists. Although perfect hips are not essential, a fair degree of fault in this area will certainly show up at some stage during a working life. Many people believe that the scale jump is the first to highlight a hip weakness, but in fact the long jump is more demanding on the hip joints and a dog will usually fail or show reluctance to try the long jump before the failure to scale becomes apparent.

Educating Your Alsatian

With a dog at any age the first day in his new home is the time to start the educational partnership. The owner will study and learn the mannerisms of his dog and then the dog will learn to become socially acceptable. Education commences by avoiding situations where the dog is likely to disobey your requirements. Remember, it takes time for him to understand what you want. This approach will, of course, continue throughout the rest of his life. If you expect disobedience do not try to exert authority. This may sound negative, but the secret of willing and faithful compliance with your wishes is to ensure that your dog understands and enjoys obeying your requests. Your approach must always be tempered to suit your dog's mental maturity.

A new owner can find himself with a young puppy straight from the nest, or an older pup, say eight to twelve months acquired from the breeding kennel, or even a junior coming into his second home. These differing circumstances create different settling-in problems.

Young puppies take time to develop their minds and only a very simple progressive form of training along with social education should be given to an age of five or six months. However, a great deal of conditioning can be carried out during these early months in preparing for an actively controlled future as an adult. During this early stage of his puppy life he should appreciate the security of your company and you should build up for his loyalty in the future. Your puppy should realise the need for immediate response to your call and should also recognise that these destructive little ventures of chewing at will are just 'not on'. Education in the early stages is mainly the prevention of bad habits.

The New Puppy

What better than planning the acquisition of a little eight-week-old puppy, especially when you have looked around and decided that the parents of your new charge are satisfactory – of good temperament and sound construction? Dog or bitch puppy, it is your choice. Throughout this book, for convenience, I use the male gender to suit both sexes unless the item relates to a particular sex.

The decision of his name may not seem to be particularly important, but I feel that it is nice to be reasonably original, and I find that the choice of name can make a difference to his reaction when called. At least one strong-sounding syllable, and used strongly, can gain immediate attention. I think the strong accent of a Scottish voice can have an advantage over some of the more mellow English accents. My first Alsatian was Quest, and because the strong Dundee accent cultivated to overcome the noise of jute weaving looms could produce a very penetrating 'E', Quest had no excuse for not hearing his name.

Bringing the puppy home from the kennels also requires some thought and planning. First, there is every possibility that it will be his first journey in a car, bus or train, and you can expect him to be sick, so go well prepared with newspapers and towels. This problem can possibly be avoided by visiting your veterinary surgeon for a suitable mild tranquilliser to sedate your puppy before you start that long journey home. Although Sunday afternoon may seem to be a convenient time to collect a new puppy, it does not give the man of the house much opportunity to get to know his pup during the first vital days. If the pup is to become Mum's dog and she is at home all week with him, then time of collection does not matter so much.

Each dog I have owned has been trained for working trials, and the arrival of each one to our household was arranged to give me at least a few days at home before settling back to the usual routine of going to work in the morning and returning in the evening. There was, however, one exception, Tanya. Due to circumstances beyond our control, my wife had to go to the airport to collect Tanya on a Friday afternoon, bring her home in the train, and spend the weekend and then the whole of the following week looking after this puppy before I had a real opportunity to get to know her. This was the one dog who continued to show first preference to my wife during the whole of her life. With all the time I spent training her, Tanya continued to give my wife her first loyalty.

If a puppy is to be fully trained by a particular member of the family then that person should be 'number one' in the eyes of the puppy from the first day in his new home.

During the first few weeks a puppy can do no wrong. He may well do things that do not suit you, like chewing slippers, socks and all the other sweet-smelling bits and pieces left lying around by us humans in our careless manner, or he may soil the carpet because his toilet requirements were not anticipated.

This, therefore, brings us to the first stage of social education.

Prevention and understanding are much more effective than attempts at correction after the event. If we consider a puppy's toilet requirements, the critical times are immediately after eating and after sleeping, so these are the times when a puppy should be taken out into the garden to perform.

This is where the first association of place and performance becomes effective. Every 'accident' in the house indicates a lack of the correct association. The more often you fail to take the puppy to the toilet area in time the less chance there is of building up the required association, and 'accidents' will continue to happen. An extension of this toilet area association will be achieved by verbal encouragement, such as 'Clean boy, hurry up.' This encouragement will eventually help to induce the desired performance where and when it is found to be convenient.

If there is any thought of punishment for 'accidents' by smacking or nose rubbing in the soiled area this could be reserved for the owner and not the puppy. After all it was the owner's fault for not anticipating the situation.

Correct and timely associations should be the main form of education for a young puppy. Whilst a puppy is in the act of sitting ask him to sit. When he is in the act of lying down ask him to go down. If he is going to bed of his own accord then ask him to go to bed. The most important association of all is to call your puppy when he is coming to you. If you see that it is his purpose to come to you then call him in. Future training will be much easier with the back-up of these planned early associations.

Young puppies require plenty of rest and they know themselves when to sleep and for how long. A puppy's sleeping habits should be recognised and respected. A puppy who is continually woken up and fussed over may well mature into an edgy dog. Just consider how bad-tempered humans can be when woken up. Puppies, like young babies, should be given the opportunity to sleep to suit their own requirements.

Travel sickness can sometimes be quite a problem with a young puppy but the sooner a youngster gets used to car travelling the easier it is to overcome the problem. Although a puppy should not be taken out in public until he is clear of injections, he can be taken for short runs in the car to get him used to travelling. In fact a quiet seat in a stationary car can get him used to his surroundings and may well help to make him a better traveller.

It will now be appreciated that the first few weeks in his new home are possibly the most important of his life. This is the time when a relationship is going to be moulded. It may help if it can be remembered that during this period the objective is to prevent problems from arising and not to spend your time scolding him for 'misbehaviour'. It is understandable that a puppy will get bored and will look around for his own forms of enjoyment. His enjoyment may be a good chew at a favourite slipper or suchlike. Rather than scold him it is much more sensible to distract him from the object in question and attract his attention to one of his own toys. The first thing I have ready for a new puppy coming into my home is a knitted jersey or cardigan, minus buttons or zips. This is his tug-of-war article and comforter; it always goes to bed with him and every time I catch him doing something I do not want I get the jersey, call him from the scene of the 'crime', and then we have fun with it. I think my Callum was on his fifth jersey when he was two and a half years old and qualified P.D. Ex. If I said to him: 'Where's your jersey?' he would stop, think, then disappear. He would return with the jersey looking for some fun.

Taking Home a Junior

This may be a young dog past the small puppy stage, say from five months onwards to a full junior having lived more than a year of his life before joining your family, and during this period he may have had the opportunity to pick up many undesirable habits. His earlier life may have been totally within the breeding kennel or he may have come to you from another home.

In either case he should be given time to settle and develop some sense of security with his new owner. The initial few days are very important, with the first week being used to gain his confidence.

The older puppy straight from a breeding kennel can create his share of problems. With a maturing mind he will take time to settle in, perhaps three months to settle fully into his changed environment. In all probability he has not known the fun that more constant companionship can give, nor will he have experienced the effects of living in the so-called civilised community. He may also have picked up bad habits during kennel life. Kennel staff do not always have the time or the patience to put up with troublesome little puppies who do not wish to go back to their kennels, or will not be caught to be shut away last thing at night, especially when the kennel maid has a boyfriend waiting. These are factors one never hears or knows about, and they can have a great deal of effect on approach to educating your new charge.

With the older pup or junior dog, coming into his second home, we consider this as the second change in the youngster's life, remembering that he probably went from a breeding kennel into his first home. Temperament and character can play a big part in his ability to settle in, and again patience is probably required to help him through his period of uncertainty. It is not uncommon for a youngster to take three to four months to settle in fully and great care should be taken with his education and training during this period.

We hear many stories as to why owners wish to part with a young dog, but unfortunately the truth is seldom told. There is generally something wrong with the dog, or should I say that he has probably acquired faults through his previous owner's lack of knowledge or consideration. The new owner must learn to recognise the problems associated with his youngster and patiently set about correcting them as part of the dog's education.

34

In general the new owner is competing against a mature and experienced mind, one that already knows most of the little dodges so easily acquired by a dog not suitably disciplined. The owner's objective is to be one move ahead of the dog and be ready to prevent or counter any unsatisfactory habit.

Making Your Dog Socially Acceptable

To be socially acceptable a dog must be controlled, but it should also be evident that he enjoys life to the full. There is no pleasure in owning a dog who does not know how to enjoy himself, but he must be prepared to accept you, his owner, as 'number one'. If you are the true 'pack leader' you will have his loyalty and respect and will also find that he enjoys his controlled form of freedom. On the other hand if he becomes the 'pack leader' your life can be one of misery. He will not lead a better life and will certainly be considered socially unacceptable by others.

I think there are three main conditions to consider as targets when achieving a socially acceptable dog:

1   He is easy to live with.
2   His manners are admired and he is accepted by neighbours.
3   He is controlled in a manner that will minimise the possibility of injury or death by accident.

Many of the problems I am asked about by troubled owners can be difficult to cure, especially those occurring when the owner is not present or is caught unprepared. Some of the cures require expert handling and timing. It is easy for the expert to advise but it is often too much to ask the average owner to apply these cures. However, many problems can be prevented, and a little thought or anticipation can overcome most of the bad habits already acquired by a dog.

At home, my own bitch Jeza is one of the greatest kitchen pedal-bin rakers of all time, especially when she is on a diet. To stop this would probably require a set-up that would automatically frighten her from the bin every time she went to lift up the lid with her nose. As she only misbehaves in this manner when we are out of the house for a lengthy period it is much simpler to put the bin out of her reach. In this case prevention is easier than correction. If I forget to put the bin out of reach and return home to find eggshell, potato peelings etc. all over the kitchen floor I only have myself to blame.

If your dog is a car chaser, why let him out on the street? Anyway, he should not be out on the street without a leash. If he is a fence jumper, why let him out in the garden without a suitable means of control? If the problem has become a habit then prevent the opportunity, and if it is serious enough take measures to correct the fault. Anticipate the problem, take preventative measures or corrective action.

One problem I had with Callum as a youngster was his aversion to stray dogs coming into the front garden. Callum normally had the freedom of the back garden and the gate was level with the front of the house. This gate was of open spars and about two and a half feet high. He never made any attempt to jump this gate but would put his front paws on the top when welcoming me home from work, and I did not discourage him. Twice, however, Callum decided to take exception to a stray dog in his front garden, jumped over the gate and gave chase across the road into a field. This could easily have caused a bad road accident and could not be permitted to continue. Thereafter he was never allowed to place his paws on the top of the gate. When I came home in the evening, as soon as his paws touched the top of the gate I hit them hard with my hands. This hurt him, and it was rough justice when you consider that I did not discourage him at earlier dates. He had to be taught very fast and in a positive manner to prevent any recurrence of the previous two chases. The treatment was effective and Callum never jumped the gate again. This was one instance where a forceful solution was used to correct my earlier failing and had to be used to minimise the risk of an accident.

Forceful solutions to problems should not become a habit,

but there are occasions when they are the most effective.

There are occasions when various preventative measures are required to overcome a problem. Take the problem of the canine thief – we are, of course, speaking about the dog who steals food. This is a very common problem and I am sure many stories have been told of Sunday dinners and suchlike which have gone missing.

My own daughter's lovable little bitch Dornie demolished about two dozen Christmas pies which were thought to be in a safe place. Then there was Rowdy, who disposed of an uncooked chicken which had just been taken out of the refrigerator. He was subsequently fed with cotton wool soaked in milk. The cotton wool became wrapped round the chicken bones to assist with an easier and less damaging passage. We also had our own Callum, who at eleven months old discovered the butcher had left the garage door open after delivering a frozen ox head. By the time the head was about five pounds short of its normal weight Callum was found with his prize. Callum must have had an iron constitution because this gorging of frozen meat did not seem to cause him any real discomfort. I remember another called Chuffy, who was only about eight months old when a newly-baked cake went missing with only a few crumbs to show that it had ever existed. When confronted with this evidence Chuffy looked at his owner's twins in an attempt to divert the blame, but as the twins were barely at the crawling stage Chuffy had no hope of getting out of that situation.

There are many cases of stolen morsels, and most of these cases are due to human thoughtlessness. Some dogs will steal at every opportunity and others will only do so when they are severely tempted. Only the owner can determine the magnitude of his problem and apply the necessary self-discipline to ensure that opportunities are not available for his dog to thieve.

There are, of course, times when a more forceful attitude must be applied when a dog shows interest in forbidden food. A very short and instantaneous use of the voice will be required, and if this proves to have insufficient effect a smack on his hindquarters can be used to let him know you mean business. Do not pull him away but call him from the food and make sure that he does not get the opportunity to regain interest in this particular item. To scold the dog after he has helped himself to food is rather late and will probably be of little value. A scolding may relieve your own feelings, but at the dog's expense. The dog owner can do a great deal to prevent food stealing, and by anticipation can educate and assist his dog to overcome the temptation.

Food refusal is a completely different problem and, if considered by the owner to be a necessity, should not be confused with the educational requirements to prevent stealing. I have been asked on occasions about training for food refusal and have found it difficult to understand the desire to put a pet dog through this form of training, which is very much against the dog's nature, as there is no inherited instinct to work on. The only justification I can see for the owner of a pet dog wishing to teach him to refuse food is the genuine fear of deliberate poisoning.

I have trained only two of my own dogs for food refusal and this was purely for the Police Dog Stake in working trials. The training was geared to the conditions one would expect when competing, but it meant that friends could not give these dogs tit-bits.

By its nature training for food refusal is unpleasant for the dog. We are creating unpleasant associations under particular circumstances, and any time unpleasant associations are being created great care must be taken to ensure that the correct associations are forming in the dog's mind. It is too easy to introduce unwanted side-effects. It should be recognised that a pet owner cannot train a dog to refuse food under practical conditions without outside assistance in the shape of an experienced helper, preferably a stranger to the dog. For simplicity and reliability any training should be limited to the circumstances and localities where the poisoned food is liable to be left.

I remember one police dog handler who trained his dog to refuse food from everybody but himself. He was so successful that the day he went into hospital his dog stopped eating and even refused the food offered by the handler's wife. The answer was to bring the dog's meal to the hospital each day and have the handler spend the visiting period squeezing the food through his fingers so that the food contained a high concentration of his scent. This was the only way found to get the dog to eat.

Code of Good Manners

Preventing bad habits from taking a firm hold is the responsibility of the dog owner, and most bad habits can be avoided by the recognition of a code of good manners. The application of such a code will go a long way to making our dogs socially acceptable.

The Code

1   Some people love dogs and others hate them. There is no need to try and convert the dog lovers but respect for the views of others can only help to convert them in the long term.
2   A dog should *never* be out on the street on his own. The temptation to investigate the outside world and become one of a pack can be very great. The stray dog is gun fodder for the 'dog haters'.
3   Keep your dog on the lead until you reach a suitable exercise area. There is nothing clever about taking a dog for a walk without a lead. Another loose dog may cause a fight, a cat may cause him to dart on to the road. It only requires a passing motorcar and the prospect of human and canine tragedy is very real.
4   When your dog is free in an exercise area keep an eye on him, especially if another dog comes into view. The other dog may be a fighter, and experience has taught us that the Alsatian always gets the blame.

5 Do not let your dog soil the pavement or a public place. Give him the opportunity at the right time and in the right place and there will then be little chance of an accident.

6 A walk on the lead should not be a constant battle between dog and owner, with the dog constantly trying to pull his owner's arm out of the socket. Although there is no need for obedience-style heel work when out for a walk, the dog should be taught to walk on a 'loose' lead. The first training element of the recall exercise should be very helpful in gaining the correct measure of control.

7 Your dog must respond to the recall when instructed, not as an obedience exercise but as an essential form of control.

8 Your dog should be taught to go down immediately where and when instructed. In an emergency this may be more necessary than the recall.

9 Your dog should always be prepared to accept a reasonable measure of control and when young children or elderly people are around it may be advisable to keep him on a lead. A boisterous dog can so easily knock the very young or elderly down. Children can become frightened of dogs for life and the elderly are very prone to injury.

10 Rough games with a dog can be enjoyable, but can be a dangerous form of amusement if the dog is not under sufficient control to stop when required.

11 Do not let your dog become overprotective, either of yourself or of his food. He should be quite prepared to accept strangers, although he does not have to welcome them. He should never be permitted to show signs of aggression when he is eating.

12 Do not tolerate unnecessary barking. If he is telling you that somebody is approaching, tell him how good he is then distract him from the cause. If the barking continues then forceful action is required.

13 Do not let your dog jump up to welcome people. If you and your friends get down to his level when he comes to welcome you the habit of jumping up can be avoided.

14 Do not let your dog jump out of the car in an uncontrolled manner. It is preferable to train him to wait until after the door has been opened, then call him out when you are ready. This may well prevent an accident.

15 Always be on the lookout for faults developing. An amusing situation with a puppy can develop into a very serious problem as he matures.

16 Respect the farmer's land and livestock. You may know that your dog will not cause problems but there is no need to worry the farmer.

17 Teach yourself and your dog the elements of control (see Chapters 3 and 4).

Chapter Three

Approach to Training

The Basis for Training

Very few Alsatian puppies are non-starters for a life of obedient companionship or for work in the field of obedience competition or working trials, although their upbringing and conditioning for adult life can affect their full potential.

A lot of effort, worry and plain hard graft can be prevented by conditioning a puppy for an obedient future. A puppy can enjoy the early part of his life and may well enjoy it more if he is given the opportunity to follow and respect his 'pack leader' – that is, you, the handler. A puppy should experience authority, fairness and also the great excitement of life. All these can be experienced in preparing him for a happy and faithful future.

Initial training of any puppy must be based on two requirements:

1   his respect for you, which can only be based on his happy desire to please you;
2   the prevention of bad habits.

He should give his immediate attention to you, no matter what he is doing, when commanded. He must also be prepared to come to you when called, and he should learn the need for a prompt response to this request.

It should be noted that *commands* are used to obtain immediate attention, and *requests* are used to achieve something positive and active. I shall be going into the philosophy of this approach and it will be seen that this concept of control and training is based on the command and request. A request does not mean that you accept a refusal or allow time to think about it. It means that your tone of voice is that of a request, with your actions that of urgency and excitement.

An example of this approach to training is getting a puppy to come when called. There should never be a need to teach a puppy to come in the formal sense of the expression. He should be conditioned to want to be with you when he is called with the sole objective of an immediate response. This can best be achieved if the puppy has a genuine desire to be with you and if there is something to come back for, something much more interesting than the thought taking his attention when called.

I have found the best way to condition a very young puppy initially is just to give him a flick or tap on the hindquarters with a finger when he is going away from me – this, of course, is whilst he is under no control and free to do what he wants. When giving this flick I call his name and he will turn his head to see what is wanted – remember he is only a few feet from me. I then make a great thing of him coming back and let him know he is really wanted. He must feel that it is good to be with me or that something great is going to happen.

In using this approach you must make your puppy feel that something is going to happen when he comes in to you. Sometimes you give him plenty of love and affection, sometimes you make it fun and games, and on other occasions make it a nice juicy titbit. Whatever you do, vary your response to his return, make it worth his while and let him think, what is it going to be this time? The secret of initial training is to have him want to come back to you. The request to come is the signal for something pleasant.

This approach can be built on by eventually allowing a little more distance between yourself and your puppy. At this stage do not call him when his attention is on something, do not create a clash of desires until he is fully responsive to your call when little appears to be on his mind. At no time do you move towards your puppy once you have called him; if anything move away and draw him in with plenty of excitement and encouragement.

Commands, and with a stern tone of voice, are used to stop him from doing something and should be of the severity required to achieve the objective. The command may only be to get his attention so that the recall request can be given. The command, however, should not be given until you are in a position to enforce it, or from past experience are guaranteed an immediate response. The 'in my own time' attitude at this stage is out of the question. In general the 'command' need only be the use of the puppy's name.

Although the correct approach to the conditioning and upbringing of a puppy is most important, it does not mean to say that all is lost if a young or adult dog has not had the benefit of this start in life. It may well mean a lot more hard work on the part of the handler to retrieve the situation. It is much easier to be patient with a young puppy than with a young dog or adult, especially if by then you are correcting your own earlier failings, as there is a strong tendency to blame the dog for the faults that have developed. There can also be the feeling that time has been lost and must now be made up for the correction of these faults. Short-cuts in training must not be confused with efficient training. Efficient training may appear to be the long way round, but it is built on a solid foundation with sound long-lasting results, and this approach is usually quicker in the long run. Short-cuts lead to all sorts of troubles. They may, if you are good enough, get you through a show or trials, but in most cases we find that the dog is only half-trained. His handler usually says: 'That worked,' and continues to build on the temporary success only to wonder why failure or poor performances follow later on.

Efficient training is dependent on a sound approach with a

capable and understanding handler, and any training method is only as good as the trainer's ability to pass it on and also the handler's ability to apply it.

A dog will learn through habit or conditioning, from encouragement, reward or displeasure; he will also learn through his desire to please you. An Alsatian will only satisfy that desire if he knows that you are pleased and he will certainly know that something is wrong when he thinks you are displeased. The point is, will he know what you are displeased about?

The biggest mistake which many owners make is expecting their dog to think and reason as a human. A dog does not reason as a human being, although a highly-trained dog may well appear to do so. Dogs learn through habit, they learn from the pleasant and also from the unpleasant.

The best example one can give is that of the dog who will not come back when called and when he eventually does come back is given a telling off, or a hiding for staying away. In fact, the dogs thinks that he is being punished for coming back, because that was the last thing he did. He relates the pleasant and the unpleasant with his last action. Under these circumstances the next time he is called he remembers he got a hiding the last time, and will be reluctant to return. If the handler maintains this approach the dog will become more and more reluctant to come back when called.

You may well be saying: What is the answer? The answer to that particular problem is given in the training for the recall. The main point is, however, that you should remember he will relate your response to his last action. This is the most important principle in dog training.

What does a dog trainer mean by conditioning, habit, encouragement, rewarding or displeasure? This is my interpretation:

Conditioning means preparing a dog for the exercise or element, building him up in a manner which will lead to the reaction you require.

Habit is the repetition of an element of an exercise in such a way that it will become a natural function and in a manner the dog enjoys.

Encouragement is the verbal and physical support given to the dog in assisting him to carry out the element or exercise.

Reward is the spontaneous pleasure you show when he responds to your wishes. This may, of course, be reinforced by the use of titbits on completion of the task.

Displeasure should only be 'the sharp edge of your tongue' if you do not receive the instant or correct response to your wishes. This is, of course, when training is sufficiently advanced for him to know that he is doing wrong. There may well be occasions when more drastic action is required when the dog is beside you. There is nothing more effective than taking two handfuls of loose skin at his neck and giving a three-second blast with your tongue whilst you are looking him straight in the eye (or as I have heard it put, 'having a little word in his ear'). This sort of treatment should not really be necessary, but if used it should immediately be followed by something exciting that you know will achieve the correct response.

Commands, Instructions and Requests

'Giving commands' in dog training is an expression that is generally used and applied. Everything seems to be based on giving commands for this, that, and the next thing. Go to a training club, read most books on training, and it is the same – working a dog to commands. So long as we continue to use this word freely we shall think that way and tend to train that way. Many people, however, realise that it is just a figure of speech.

If we consider our life in industry, commerce, or with the family at home, how unbearable it would be if all instructions were carried out to commands. We would then find that there would be many a rebellion or we would become immune to this approach. Life is normally much more acceptable because we are usually *requested* to carry out our functions, and in the main these requests are just commands dressed up to maintain a pleasant and cooperative atmosphere.

As our dogs are obedient companions or working partners we should not require to give them commands to carry out what should be a pleasant task, but dogs, like children, need to be controlled, instructed and encouraged to obey instructions, and yet enjoy life to the full. It is therefore preferable to think of instructions and requests than of commands. If you keep in mind that you wish to finish with a happy dog, one who is very keen to please you, a dog who knows you appreciate everything that he does for you, the main consideration is to use an approach which creates a real desire to please.

Before discussing the replacement for the command approach I would like to go into the response we expect from a trained dog, for it is a reflection of our own attitude to training. If we are demanding and lacking in consideration we may have a dog who does as he is told but is probably devoid of character. If we are firm but fair, happy and full of encouragement, constructing our training in such a manner that the dog enjoys these sessions, we should finish with an eager dog full of character.

We want to train in a manner which releases the dog to carry out our requests. If we want him to retrieve we should not find it necessary to give him a command and send him for the article; we want to be in a position to release him so that his great desire takes him out to get this article and bring it quickly back. If we do a 'send away', again we wish to release him to go out in the direction that has been indicated. Every active movement is a release from a closely controlled situation.

If you think this way, you can train this way.

When you want to obtain a dog's undivided attention or have him remain in a stationary position (i.e. creating a static situation) you instruct him, and there should just be sufficient edge in your voice to achieve the desired effect. When you want to create an active situation you request him to do it. As training develops you may well find your instructions become less frequent and requests will achieve the reaction that you are after.

Now we are thinking in terms of instructions and requests. Instructions in varying degrees of firmness may be used to obtain attention or create a closely controlled static situation. Requests are used to release him to carry out a controlled exercise.

Training Elements

Everything we teach a dog can be broken down into elements, or even sub-elements. If we take the simplest action in asking a dog to sit, this can be broken into three elements, each one as important as the other. These elements are: obtaining the dog's undivided attention; getting him to sit; and keeping him in the sit position. It will be obvious that getting a dog to sit on request is not practical if his undivided attention cannot be obtained, and it is a waste of time getting him to sit if you cannot get him to stay in that position for a short period of time. This is a very elementary exercise for any dog, and it may appear to be very simple. It can be achieved by the overbearing and domineering approach, or the dog can find it to be a pleasing function because it makes his boss happy. The overbearing approach may achieve the result you wish but it is a poor beginning if you wish later to control him at a distance, and even with the companion dog it is essential to obtain control at a distance.

Each element of an exercise or sub-element is *static* or *active*. The static elements are those which stop a dog from doing something, such as getting the dog's attention or maintaining an inactive position. The active elements are those which require the dog to do something. Let us now consider the elements of the sit exercise. They are:

48

1   Obtaining the dog's undivided attention: a static element which until the dog understands is taken as an instruction. The instruction may only be the use of the dog's name with an urgent tone of voice. The dog's name can be used as an instruction to pay attention.

2   Getting the dog to sit: an active element, requesting, encouraging and helping the dog to go into the sit position.

3   Keeping him in the sit position: another static element. This requires firm instruction with a soothing appreciation for obeying the instruction. In this instance his name is not the dominant word although the instruction to sit-stay is applied with the firmness required to maintain this static situation. To keep a dog inactive for a period of time requires a great deal of concentration from the handler during the initial training stage. The handler should use his voice as a steadying influence and give the dog full assurance that he is doing fine, but he must be ready with a sharp instruction if there is any inclination to move.

Another requirement that can be considered essential for any dog is to come back when called. This again has three elements:

1   Obtaining the dog's undivided attention: a static element, this probably lasts for a split second until you have given the call to come immediately back to you. Without his undivided attention there is not a hope of achieving Element 2.

2   Getting him to come back to you immediately and smartly: an active element that requires all the encouragement you can muster to create in him the habit of returning when called. This should be applied as an excited request to return. Any attempt to use a firmly voiced instruction will result in a reluctant return or even a complete refusal to come in when called.

3   Staying with you willingly: a calm and reassuring situation follows in keeping the dog quietly inactive

until you have had time to tell him how good he is and also to clip on his lead.

As a handler your own actions and the correct use of your voice will create the static and active situations which the various elements require. This comment is just as important for the companion dog owner as for the working dog owner.

Breaking Down Exercises Into Elements

Every exercise can be broken down into a number of elements as indicated above, and with consideration for the static or active functions most elements can be broken into sub-elements. If we take teaching a dog to sit as part of a full exercise, such as the recall, then this becomes an element of the recall with the previous example showing the three parts as sub-elements.

If we take the recall as an exercise it can be broken down into the following elements:

1 Stay when told until recalled by handler.
2 Come directly to handler when called.
3 Sit squarely in front of handler.
4 Go smartly round to heel to finish the exercise.

As we have already seen, element (1) can be broken into three sub-elements: (a) pay attention; (b) sit; (c) stay sitting. We can now take the complete exercise and break it down fully to show the various static and active situations.

Recall

Element	Sub-Element	Classification
1 Stay till called.	Obtaining dog's attention.	Static.
	Getting dog to sit.	Active.
	Keeping him in sit position whilst you leave him.	Static.
2 Recall to handler.	Maintaining attention for recall.	Static.

	Recall and return of dog	
	to handler.	Active.
3 Sit in front of	Sit in front.	Active.
handler.	Remain sitting.	Static.
4 Round to heel.	Maintaining attention	
	for the final step.	Static.
	Round to heel on request.	Active.
	Sit at handler's side.	Active.
	Remain sitting.	Static.

It will be seen that even with this simple exercise there are eleven different situations for the dog, requiring six changes by handler as he controls the dog from static to active or active to static situations. Each change requires a change in the tone of voice, a change in attitude of mind, a change from subdued attention to immediate activity and then back again to subdued attention. A handler must think this way and act this way to obtain the most effective and efficient response from the dog.

Every exercise should be broken down in this manner. Many experienced handlers do this without thinking very much about it – the process has become second nature to them. When breaking down an exercise into elements consider which one to teach first and whether various elements should be taught quite separately from each other but in parallel, so that they may be dovetailed together later when being executed to satisfaction. The full process of this form of teaching is given in the chapters for each individual exercise. The companion dog owner should note that the same basic principle applies for any normal domestic control.

Conditioning for an Element

We have already discussed the need to consider and treat each element separately, so we can now go into the preparation for each element or sub-element. Conditioning is really another word for controlled anticipation.

Without anticipation we could not train a dog.

A dog will show us dozens of examples of his anticipation every day, and if we study the causes we can understand how a dog is such a trainable creature. For instance, take his feeding dish out of the cupboard at a particular time of day and he knows he is going to be fed – he anticipates the event. Put on your walking shoes last thing at night and he anticipates his final chance of the day for exercise. Close the car tailgate on his ear or tail and see what happens the next time the tailgate is closed: he anticipates trouble. It may take a few uneventful closures of the tailgate before he anticipates that no harm will come to him. Yet if he is a sensitive dog or he has got a really nasty nip he may always anticipate it happening and keep away from the tailgate and never give it the chance to inflict such pain again.

Anticipation must be turned to our advantage: if we can have the dog anticipating our every intention we have achieved a tremendous understanding. However, like everything else we use to our advantage it must be controlled – that is why I have used the phrase 'controlled anticipation'. This anticipation can be used to build up the power behind his desire to carry out the function he knows is coming, and your actions or the way you speak to him will tell him what is coming next. As a result of the correct application of habit and routine he anticipates the next move and enjoys it. If he does not enjoy the next move you will soon know by his reaction, for the way he anticipates it will make it obvious that your method of conditioning has not been pleasant to him.

Training Sequence

If we accept that the foundation training given in Chapter 4 is the first essential, and that training for an immediate response to basic control is top priority, we can then think beyond the foundation training exercises and move on to the more advanced stages.

The question then is, do we concentrate on a very small number of exercises for a quick return or do we tackle a broader field for a slower long-term return? Although I feel that there is only one answer, there must be a good sound reasoning behind it. This comes down to our own mental approach to training rather than the dog's ability to cover a broad field at the one time. If we tackle one or two exercises fully and look for perfection in their execution, we start with the feeling that with a fair amount of concentration it should not take long to get the dog licked into shape. With this approach it is all too easy to become impatient, to have excessive determination, and to feel that time is slipping by without the expected response from the dog. There can be a tendency to move on from one element to the next without consolidating the work previously carried out. There can also be a tendency to spend too long within each session on too few elements, thereby creating boredom.

If we now consider the full range of training exercises beyond the foundation group, we should again break them down into elements and decide on the initial training element for each exercise. We should look for those initial training elements that are natural for a dog, so that we may not even need to wait until the foundation training is complete before starting with some of them. It is much easier to pick out the natural elements in training for working trials than for obedience competitions.

A number of exercises which can be started by early conditioning and have elements which are natural to the dog are:

1 The agility tests. It is quite natural for a dog to jump if he wishes. So long as heights are kept to the minimum, even with a four-month-old puppy we can have great fun conditioning him so that the scale jump with one six-inch board becomes so enjoyable that he looks forward to it. Similarly jumping over a single board from the long jump lays a good foundation for this exercise

later. The clear jump can be laid down flat and the puppy have fun charging over it. All this can be done to condition him and prepare for serious training at a later date.

2 Speak on request. What is more natural than a puppy or dog barking? If we encourage but control this barking from the very start we can make life so much easier for ourselves. This should be a 'must' for all house dogs.

3 Tracking. Another exercise that can be conditioned at an early age, but the chapter on tracking should be studied and the various pitfalls appreciated before steaming ahead.

Although the above can be considered as 'natural' exercises which can be trained along with the foundation group, almost any exercise can be started with the sound basis of our foundation group.

A dog enjoys variety in training. Boredom by repeating the same thing time and time again is his greatest enemy. Many dogs make progress even on a poor foundation and with an impatient handler, but few of them reach the top of the ladder, and it is generally found that such dogs are working to please their handler through fear.

Basic Requirements for all Training

Before starting with the foundation training exercises described in the following chapter there are a few basic requirements that a handler should appreciate before going into the training of any one exercise. These are as follows:

1 *Handler attention.* If you want hundred per cent attention from your dog you must be prepared to give this to him during training. He is entitled to your full attention – any failure on your part will result in failure on his. This being so, keep the sessions short but intensive whilst they last.

2 *Voice control.* Probably the most important thing for a handler to learn is how to use his or her voice to obtain

the right response from the dog. Any sharpness used to get his attention must be short and snappy with an immediate softening of tone afterwards and with the recall an excited tone to encourage the dog to come in. A sharp tone of voice should only be used to get the dog's attention and at no other time. If this sharpness of tone is not successful on the first call then your training is not soundly based. Continual shouting is of little value in successful dog training.

3 *Body and hand control.* It can be of great value to use body and hand movements as signals, but you must be conscious of their useful application. The proper and natural use of signals will help your dog, so long as you know you are using them. You can later minimise these signals or cut them out when no longer needed. Hand and arm signals in particular can be used to reinforce acts of encouragement.

4 *Use of food as reward.* Titbits of food should never be used in place of other forms of reward or encouragement, but rather to back up or reinforce encouragement and praise. The correct use of food can have a dramatic effect on the progress of training and should not be discarded as unnecessary in dog training. To obtain the best results in training, a dog should never be fed before a training session – it is much easier to train a hungry dog. A training session just before feeding time where titbits are used to reinforce praise and encouragement can prove to be very effective. It should be noted that training without titbits can restrict the effectiveness of repeating that part of an exercise to about three to five tries before moving to another part. After this a dog normally loses his edge and the handler wonders why performance deteriorates. However, the use of titbits can prolong a session for twenty to thirty repeats with a very hungry dog. The idea is to get the right balance and really understand your dog's limitations.

Dogs can be and are trained very effectively without ever using a titbit. But my belief is that, as an aid, the use of food can speed up and help consolidate on the elements being trained. Also, the use of titbits can help to keep the handler in a better frame of mind. What handler can be coarse and overbearing whilst he is giving his dog something to eat? It just would not make sense.

Remember, do not overdo any training session.

Chapter Four

The Foundation Exercises

General

The first aim of every Alsatian owner must be to achieve complete control with instant response to his wishes. Whether the dog is to remain a companion or be trained with a broader field in mind, every dog should know who is boss, and at the same time he should have complete trust in his master. He should respect and obey, but he should also experience fun and enjoyment such as any child can expect from his parents.

The basis for this companionship and the foundation for further training can best be attained through the training of the foundation exercises. Precision may only be required for competition work but instant response should be expected from all dogs at all times. Any sluggishness in response will only lead to an even more sluggish approach on the next occasion unless something is done to arrest the trend.

The recall and sit-stay training exercises help to achieve the desired control, with the retrieve helping to consolidate. The retrieve, however, is more important for development in character, for the sheer joy it can release, and the opening it creates for your canine friend's intelligence and natural working ability.

The three exercises are very closely related. We cannot teach the full recall exercise without the stay, and we cannot teach the retrieve without the recall. It is therefore my aim to go through the various elements of each of these three exercises and to show the order in which they should be taught to obtain smooth progression through the full foundation training programme.

The three exercises required by the working trials schedule for the C.D. Stake are as follows:

Recall to handler. The dog should be recalled from the 'down' or 'sit' position, the handler being as far as possible from the dog at the discretion of the judge. The dog should return at a smart pace and sit in front of the handler, afterwards going smartly to heel on command or signal; handler to await command of the judge.

Sit-Stay. The dog shall sit for a full period of two minutes, all the handlers being out of sight as far as possible from the dogs at the judge's discretion. On the handlers' return to their dogs the latter should not move from the sitting position until the judge's permission has been given. The judge may cause the dogs to be tested by sending stewards to walk among them during the exercise.

Retrieve an article to hand. The dog shall not move forward to retrieve nor deliver to hand on return until ordered by the handler on the judge's instructions. The retrieve should be executed at a fast trot or gallop without mouthing or playing with the object. After delivery the dog should return to heel.

It is best not to consider the three exercises as separate training procedures but to analyse the elements that make up each exercise and to train certain elements in parallel and also in a sequence which will give the desired results.

We should consider the recall as the key exercise for canine control with the sit-stay as a requirement for the exercise in full, and then go on to the retrieve as an extension to the recall training. Figure 1 shows the breakdown of elements, the order of training and the parallel approach with the correct timing for the connecting of each group of elements, respectively the

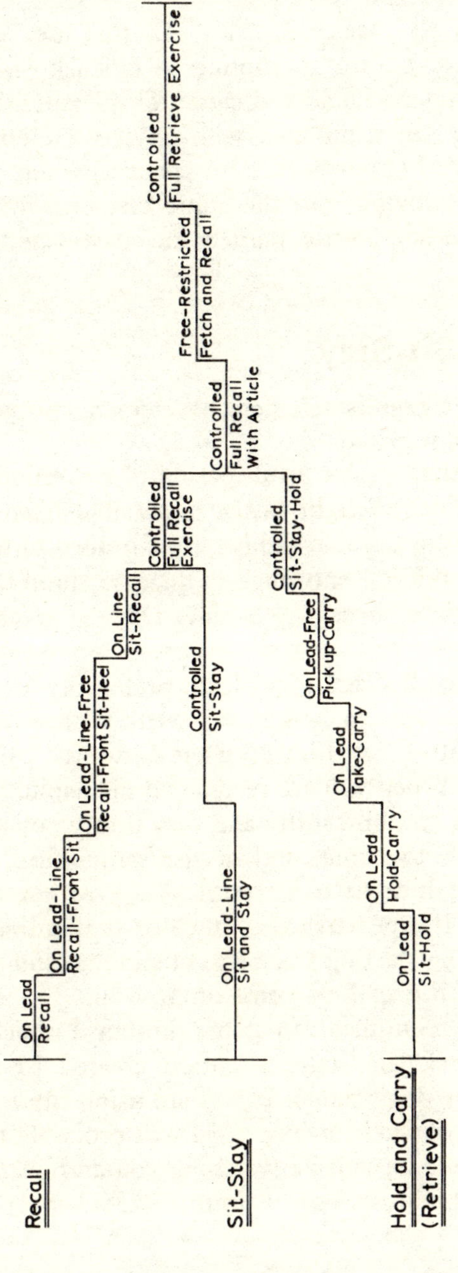

Fig. 1.   Training schedule for foundation exercises. (Time scale to suit your own requirements.)

recall, sit-stay, and hold and carry (retrieve). The first recall element should be well mastered, with hundred per cent attention from the dog, before attempting to embark on the parallel course of sit-stay and hold and carry. This ensures that both dog and handler are stimulated with an active element where there are plenty of opportunities for encouragement and excited praise before moving into the static elements which may tend to inhibit the dog a little, namely the sit-stay and the hold and carry.

The Recall and Sit-Stay

We shall now take this exercise element by element, bringing in the sit-stay at the appropriate time.

Element 1. *Come directly to handler when called.* This element should be taught with the dog on the lead, then if necessary on a long line. Progression from one stage to another should not take place until complete success is achieved at the stage in question.

Take the dog on the slip chain and lead, preferably a long one about five to seven feet in length, just walk with a loose lead and apply no control. Let him do what he wants – if he pulls you just let him. When you are ready, call his name, give a sharp tug on the lead, ask him softly and very firmly but with urgency in your voice to come, and at the same time run backwards. Encourage him to come with you, *create a real desire to be with you*. If any harshness of voice is required it should be used in calling the dog's name to obtain his attention immediately prior to the call to come in to you. The dog should not require a command to come in but rather an encouragement to break the static attention created by the sharpness in calling the dog's name. If you are using titbits let him know that you have food for him. You will probably find that in a very short time he will be watching you and waiting for the call. When his response is immediate every time

60

without a tug on the lead then change to a long line, say fifteen to twenty yards long. A strong cord will do; there is no need to use a heavy clothes line or suchlike. In fact a heavy line for control training may cause problems if you start training your dog to track.

A dog who is conditioned properly as a puppy should not require to be subjected to the long line. It is included here to ensure that you know what to do if instant response is not obtained at distances further than the length of the lead.

When using the long line give the dog complete freedom to do what he wants to do and create distance between yourself and him. The line is primarily to let him know that you still control the situation when you wish to, but it should only be used to the minimum. If response is not attained immediately on the first call of his name, then be more positive, with a sharp call of his name, and immediately call him in with a sharp tug on the line. Use all the enthusiasm you can to get him in quickly. Although you have a long line the length you make use of depends on your progress. Do not try to coil the spare line, let it drag or lie on the ground. Use your voice, hands, arms, any movement of encouragement to get a fast and effective response. Remember the following:

1   The short crisp call of his name.
2   Pleasant and soft call to 'Come'. Although soft, it should be full or urgency and encouragement.
3   Plenty of encouragement while the dog is coming in.
4   Plenty of praise for obeying the call, and titbits if these are being used.

Complete success must be attained before discarding the use of the long line. Any return to indifference on the recall must immediately be cut out by the reintroduction of the lead or line.

Element 2. *Sit square in front of handler.* The amount of effort you put into this element depends on the accuracy you want out of it. With the first element there is no question of accepting second best: immediate and purposeful response must be attained. An untidy sit in front and a sloppy finish only detract from an otherwise smart recall. But again in this element an immediate response must be obtained from your request to sit.

It is now preferable to return to the use of the slip chain and lead, returning to the start of the first element, but this time your dog knows what to expect and will be watching your every movement. When he comes in to you, move back if necessary to have him positioned straight in front of you. If you can get the dog's attention held on your face or high on your body it becomes natural for him to sit to look up. Teaching to sit for titbits can be a very useful start, especially if they are held in a position close to the body that will keep the dog's head looking up at you. In teaching the sit in front without the use of food, place one hand under the dog's lower jaw and lift his head, at the same time using the other hand to press on the croup, and giving the instruction 'Sit'. This will soon achieve results. Although you may well start this element by using compulsion and commands, the immediate follow-up of praise should soon change it from a compulsory action to one of desire to please you.

Correction to obtain a nice square sit should not require force of any kind, although a little gentle tug on the slip chain may be required as you move back a little to draw him into a closer or squarer sit position.

When this element of the exercise is to your liking it can then be applied with distance, but again it may be advisable to use the line for a period to ensure that control at a distance is obtained with the immediate response that must not be lost.

Element 3. *Smartly round to heel to finish the exercise.* This element should be taught in conjunction with a satisfactory 'sit in front', and in the early stages can be carried out at the conclusion of the recall on the lead, where full control can be maintained.

With the dog on the lead and sitting in front of you, the early stages of training are best achieved by making most of the movement yourself. This is done by taking a step to the left and forward so that the dog is behind you, when you transfer the lead round your back from right to left hand and give the instruction 'Heel'. Encourage the dog to your left-hand side and carry on walking a little further until you have full control, then make him sit nice and straight at your left hand. Again plenty of praise and titbits if required.

Continue at this stage until it becomes a fully accepted pattern. Only then do you start reducing your movement until the dog is completing the full manoeuvre without your assistance. Training the element in this way also prepares your dog for the heel work exercise.

Element 4. *Stay when told until recalled to handler*. You start by treating this as a sit-stay exercise. By way of Element 2, your dog will sit immediately when instructed. A start to sit-stay can be made as soon as Element 2 has achieved its objective.

Now concentrate on building up on time and distance. For the purpose of the recall a steady stay of half a minute at a distance of fifteen to twenty yards is sufficient. Put on the lead and use the instruction 'Stay', with a gentle signal and the flat of the hand directly in front of the dog's face. Remember it should be a gentle signal with the flat of the hand. Do not leave your dog but walk round him with the lead in hand, while you watch for indications of any movement and prevent him from lying down or trying to get up. Prevention of any mistakes in this element is extremely important, because curing them can be very difficult and wasteful of effort which could well go into constructive training. Initially keep speaking to the dog; a little sharpness in your voice should only be evident if he is thinking of moving, otherwise it is a gentle 'Stay' followed by his name. A gentle signal with the flat of the hand helps to reinforce your purpose. Do not become overconfident but build up gradually in distance and time. If you wish to use the long line in getting distance do so, but it should not be necessary. At this stage *always* go back to him. As you are teaching the stay exercise you do not want anticipation – it encourages the dog to break his stay. At this stage use the instruction 'Stay' and the hand signal.

By the time half a minute and fifteen yards give a good steady stay he will be prepared to stay with the hand signal only, and the instruction 'Stay' should not be necessary. You now start making changes to prepare for the full recall. Go back to attaching the line, and for the recall exercise change the instruction of 'Stay to 'Wait', but also use the hand signal. The instruction to 'Stay' is used when you intend to go back to him, with the instruction to 'Wait' when he is going to be recalled. Your dog, however, will now be so steady at the stay that he will not wish to move when called.

The instruction to 'Stay' should be reserved for the stay exercise when you intend to return to your dog. The use of the word 'Wait' will soon let him know that he is going to be recalled when you are ready. The stay creates a subdued state of mind in which the dog knows he can relax, but the word 'Wait' will soon prompt his anticipation of the recall to follow.

Give the instruction to 'Wait' and the hand signal as before, go out to the end of the line, have a little informal chat with him then call to come in. At the same time give a little tug on the line, create great excitement and move back. In a short time he will realise that he can break the stay when released from the 'Wait' instruction. When this happens the line can be discarded and each element will be coordinated with the others to form a very enjoyable but controlled recall.

Elementary Retrieve

Conditioning for the retrieve can be started as a game, and in fact this approach should be tried first to assess the natural responses from a puppy, or from an adult dog if training starts later.

Many dogs will retrieve, but at the same time they can develop habits which will be difficult to eradicate. When playing at retrieving it is important to watch for faults developing. Those that seem to create most problems are:

1   The dog shows a lack of interest to go out and pick up the article.
2   He goes out but is easily distracted, or he just wants to play with the article.
3   He picks up the article but runs away and plays.
4   He comes back, but in his own sweet time, mouthing and chewing it.
5   He comes back to within three to six feet of you and then runs away.

These faults are generally created by lack of foresight or just inexperienced handling. To prevent any of these problems I suggest the 'hold and carry' approach to serious training of the retrieve exercise. I shall go through the full procedure, and for your own dog it may just be a case of adapting the elements to suit your own circumstances. Remember, however, that any real training for the retrieve should only be built on a foundation of the training previously described for a good and happy recall.

Puppy playing should initially be carried out with a soft article. A soft toy, tied up sock or a glove would do, but care should be taken not to upset the puppy whilst it is teething. A problem at this stage, especially one caused by the handler, can cause a lasting reluctance to carry anything. I have seen a number of dogs that have been brutally forced to retrieve. None of them were happy, some were completely unreliable, whilst others failed to respond to this method of training.

We shall now move on to training for a competitive retrieve, but if you wish to train the retrieve for fun then extract what you wish and work within the scope of your requirements.

Before asking any dog to retrieve and give to hand he must be capable and reliable at taking, holding and carrying the article, then sitting in front of you holding it until you ask him to release the article.

The exercise should now be broken into three broad training elements:

1   Take, hold and carry.
2   Go out and fetch.
3   Return and present.

Element 3 is basically the recall training, but carrying the article. We do not consider tackling this element or the 'go out and fetch' before being sure of a sound and responsive recall. We can however, commence with the element 'take, hold and carry' as soon as the dog is under some measure of control. Probably after the satisfactory response to Element 1 of the recall exercise.

If a dog is difficult or our approach too forceful, the hardest part will be teaching him to take, hold and carry. Patience and firmness on the handler's part, together with self-control, encouragement and understanding, are most certainly the critical factors. If a dog wishes to take the article from you, and then to hold and carry it, the rest becomes relatively easy. But I do emphasise that a dog must be eager to take an article from you to hold and carry before progressing to the next stage. This, however, is one training exercise where food as a reward can be a drawback. The desire for food can cause dropping of the article, and this must be avoided at all costs.

Element 1. *Take, hold and carry.* To get your dog to hold the article, place it in his mouth, if necessary prising open his mouth and putting the article in. This is where your ability to apply patience and firmness and to change your tone of voice along with your actions can be most important. Give a firm but gentle instruction to hold and immediately follow with the 'Good dog' approach. Any attempt to spit out the article must be countered by holding his jaws gently on the article, with the instruction to hold immediately followed by praise.

The initial attempts must only last for three or four seconds;

you then take the article from him with the instruction to give. Do not let him spit it out at any time. You can probably do this three, four or five times in one training session before going on to something else more pleasant. A daily session or even two or three sessions in any one day will soon achieve good results. Always give plenty of praise when you take the article from him, and although you may appear to be rather domineering in the early stages this approach must be modified as training progresses.

The article should not be thrust into his back teeth but should be held immediately behind the canines. Once he is quite content to hold it you can start to move him around on the lead, but you may have to hold his chin up with one hand and the lead in the other. Any attempt to spit the article out must be prevented. He must understand that he is required to hold it until you take it from him. Keep the training sessions short and do not let him get bored. He will eventually find that it can be quite pleasant to hold and carry the article around. Continue until he wants to take the article from you, and if your attitude is correct this should not take long. Get him excited and try to make a game of it, but still enforce the control as it is required.

You should now be able to take him on the lead and whilst you are walking let him take the article from you. If necessary tease him a little so that he grabs it from you – this is all the better. Having done this a few times, you can now 'accidentally' drop the article when he tries to grab it from you. In the excitement he should be ready to pick it up and carry it for you. Only when this stage is reached can you start kicking the article around or throwing it a little distance, preferably whilst he is still on the lead. You can now introduce the words 'Fetch it', more as an excited request than an instruction. When he has it in his mouth use the gentle instruction 'Hold it', then 'Good boy'.

When the pick-up, hold and carry is satisfactory you can get him to sit in front and present the article to you. This should not be difficult as you will already have perfected the sit in front for the recall exercise. When you have progressed to the stage that he will pick up the article when you have been kicking it around, he will come in as you move back to draw him towards you as in the recall, and he will sit in front and present the article to you. When he does this consistently you can consider discarding the lead. The same procedure can be adopted off the lead, and only complete success at this stage will permit advancement to the full recall with the article in his mouth.

Element 3. *Return and present.* Although returning with the article and sitting in front of the handler ready for him to take it is the final main element of the exercise, it should be trained before giving the dog the freedom to 'go out and fetch'.

Carry out the full recall exercise leaving the dog in the sit-stay position with the article securely held in his mouth. If the build-up training has been carried out correctly he will come bounding in to you, sit in front and present the article. Two or three training sessions like this should be enough to ensure that no problems are going to arise when you add the 'go out and fetch' element.

Element 2. *Go out and fetch – the complete exercise.* Now you can get him excited and, with the dog off the lead, tease him a little and throw the article as far as you can. He is free to go as he pleases; no restrictions are put in his way. Give plenty of encouragement and include the words 'Fetch it'. As soon as he has the article in his mouth apply gentle control to bring him back at speed as in a normal recall. Remember that without a good sound recall your efforts will be wasted.

Your approach to date has created a situation of anticipation. Now it is more important to build up his keen desire to get that article and come straight back with it. Running out before being sent to retrieve can be corrected at the next stage in training.

Now you teach him to sit and wait before the release to go

out and retrieve the article you have thrown. Take a piece of cord seven to nine inches long and tie a knot to give a loop. Fix this loop through his slip chain, but not through the ring. You do not wish to use it as a choke chain. Put your fingers through the loop and hold – this is the start of physical restraint whilst exciting him to go out when you have thrown the article. You then release your hold as you request him to fetch the article. When he is used to this approach and really enjoys his retrieve you can make him sit and keep him sitting until you release him to go out after the article. You have built up a big bank balance and can now start drawing on it with your forceful approach in making him stay sitting until you are ready to release him. Eventually you can keep your fingers crooked in the loop attached to his slip chain, and the time will not be so far off when he understands that he should sit and wait for the verbal release to go and fetch your article. This will take a little time, but cast your mind back: you started with a dog who would not retrieve to hand and now you have one with a fully charged battery awaiting your release to do exactly what you desire.

If your training has been carried out with an article other than the dumb-bell we can combine the foundation training a little further by including the dumb-bell retrieve. It may be necessary to go back a few stages and teach the dog to hold and carry it, or on the other hand no further training may be required. It is just a case of giving a single fun retrieve with the dumb-bell to assess his reaction. It is important, however, that he carries it properly, not by the end but correctly with the centre piece immediately behind his canines.

As you want him to carry the dumb-bell by the centre piece it is essential that you too should carry and throw it by the centre piece. If your scent is stronger at the end it will only encourage your dog to pick up on the hotter scent.

Chapters 3 and 4 are probably the most important in this book for owners who wish to develop into the field of competition. Without a proper understanding of the approach to training and a successful application of the foundation exercises the more advanced work will not be tackled in a manner which will achieve an efficient or successful conclusion.

At this stage many handlers are thinking of entering competitions, probably only at club level where much friendly advice will be given. Unfortunately much of this will be of a sympathetic nature, consoling the handler on the marks the dog has lost during his workout.

Many handlers are encouraged to enter competitions before they are ready. This can be a bad thing, but on the other hand if the handler is sensible and makes use of the occasion to gain experience, and applies constructive self-analysis after the event, he will then feel greater satisfaction than he would have done by accepting sympathy for a so-called failure.

I would like to give an example of critical self-analysis after a competition. This was with Taurus in the C. D. Stake at Scarborough, when we had a 'field day'. Having qualified Taurus U.D. Ex. at the same trials and feeling very full of myself, I went in to do the C.D. work. The marking was as follows:

	Possible	Actual
Heel on lead	5	5
Heel free	15	14
Send away	10	$9\frac{1}{2}$
Recall	10	10
Sit-stay	10	10
Down stay	10	10
Retrieve	10	9
Search	10	10
Scale jump	10	10
Long jump	5	$2\frac{1}{2}$
Clear jump	5	$2\frac{1}{2}$
	100	$92\frac{1}{2}$

For the total loss of $7\frac{1}{2}$ marks, who was to blame? If we go through the marks lost we can break it down and discover the main culprit.

Heel free: 14 out of 15 is good by any trials standard and I think we can share the responsibility. Send away: this was a beautiful send away, but being a little bit uncertain about his enthusiasm to do the full distance required that day I gave a little encouragement, which lost me the half mark – that was my loss. Retrieve: this was a beautiful retrieve, straight out, good clean pick and straight back until he was two yards from me, when he stopped and dropped the dumb-bell. With one word he picked up the dumb-bell for a nice finish. Stupid dog – until we think back. He had already carried out a perfect retrieve in the U.D. Stake and this fellow was accustomed to a little encouragement in training. With a second retrieve that day without any encouragement he stopped and, thinking that there was something wrong, he dropped his dumb-bell – proof that we had not consolidated on this exercise. Long jump: as the jumps were set rather close to each other, I had witnessed one dog go for the scale jump when being sent out for the long jump. I could well imagine Taurus doing the same thing so I cut his run-up to the long jump. This was obviously too much, and he failed to clear. A second attempt proved to be no problem. Clear jump: I was a little off-hand and let him go before we were ready. He failed to take the jump cleanly and knocked it flying. Again with the proper approach the second attempt was no problem and Taurus cleared it beautifully.

Therefore, out of the $7\frac{1}{2}$ marks lost I was directly responsible for the loss of $5\frac{1}{2}$ marks on the day, and I think we can put the other two marks lost down to lack of experience as a team. Still, we finished third and with another piece of experience behind us.

The only point I wish to bring home with this example is that handlers must be prepared to apply self-criticism before considering the dog to be at fault.

Chapter Five

Control Group of Exercises

General

The Kennel Club Regulations for Working Trials (S1) and for Obedience Competitions (S2) are given in Appendices 1 and 2. They were up-to-date at the time of printing, but although the nature of the tests change very little over the years it is suggested that intending competitors obtain a current copy before entering any trials or shows. These regulations should be read and digested very carefully.

As this section covers both working trials and obedience, the training approach for any exercise will be given to suit the particular branch that requires the greatest depth, and it will be evident that certain exercises are for one branch of work only.

Before going into the training of the various control exercises, I feel it would be appropriate to quote from both the Working Trials and Obedience Regulations regarding handling.

Working Trial Regulations regarding handling: 'A person handling a dog may speak, whistle or work it by hand signals as he wishes, but he can be called to order by the Judge or Judges for making unnecessary noise, and if he persists in doing so the Judge or Judges can disqualify the dog. No person shall carry out punitive correction or harsh handling of the dog.'

72

Obedience Regulations regarding handling: 'In all classes the dog should work in a happy natural manner and prime consideration should be given to judging the dog and handler as a team.'

My aim in this chapter is to continue the approach to training which will achieve results in keeping with the above regulations.

Heel Work – On and Off Lead

Most trainers consider this to be a foundation exercise. It may well be, and with a proper approach to heel work it is a very useful breaking-in exercise. However, my experience of certain training clubs using heel work as the foundation to obedience training and showing indicates that a break from the established and traditional methods is necessary.

Training for heel on lead creates a situation where the handler can completely dominate the dog's behaviour. He can be overbearing and ruthless to the extreme and finish up with a first-class heel worker but a dog of broken spirit. Although few handlers go as far as this, there are degrees of dominance that affect the dog's approach to other and more independent exercises.

Let us consider the handler who has achieved apparent success by the overbearing and ruthless approach to heel work. A foundation has now been laid for this type of approach. This handler tends to believe that he has mastered his dog, and by a domineering method. He reckons that he can continue to train the other exercises in the same manner. If he fails to meet with the success expected, then with each session of failure he reverts to heel work to restore the absolute control that he has mastered. It is the exercise he can do 'well'. This excessive heel work training inhibits the handler and dog to the extent that they are incapable of advancing into some of the more independent exercises. Handler and dog are so conditioned that every move is carried out to strict commands.

I have described an extreme condition that can be created by an obsession on heel work. It does happen, and to an extent that warrants a good hard look at the generally accepted training methods. This situation becomes very apparent when some obedience enthusiasts decide to train for or enter working trials. It has been known for a dog to run into the long jump because he was too busy watching his handler. The handler had no idea how to condition the dog to become independent enough to see the jump. Tracking is another occasion which shows up excessive heel work control. The dog thinks that the tracking line is just a long lead and waits for the commands, instructions, tugs and pulls to tell him he is right or wrong.

I remember one occasion when three obedience Class C workers were entered in a U.D. working trials stake and each one showed the effect of excessive obedience control. They were all top-flight obedience workers, but complete domination had killed any independence and initiative. As the handlers knew the starting direction of the track, they verbally pushed the dogs in the right direction. However, the dogs and handlers got completely lost before reaching the first corner. These same dogs gave a faultless display of heel work, gaining the full five out of five marks allotted to the test, but they lost practically every mark out of the 110 allotted to the track.

There are, however, dogs on record that were top-flight obedience workers who also retained their independence and initiative and proved themselves in the working trials field. This was only achieved because the handlers maintained a more appropriate balance between strict obedience control and the independent initiative that is required for a good working trials team.

As handlers, we can learn a lot more about handling techniques and self-control if we leave heel work training until the foundation exercises have been satisfactorily accomplished. The basic ingredient for good heel work is to have the dog watching your every move, and to achieve this you must be prepared to watch his every move. As complete attention is being asked from both you and your dog, the sessions of training should be short. Thirty seconds of heel work will do much more good than thirty minutes. The initial training for the recall in the foundation group will have created the situation where the dog is prepared to pay attention to you when he knows you are going to start doing work of some kind.

Loose lead walking is the preliminary step towards heel work, and short spells should be given to achieve this end. The dog is expected to walk at your left-hand side without pulling, and has to ignore all distractions.

There is no need to start from the customary sit position at this stage – no need even to use the instruction 'Heel'. If you go back to Element 1 of the recall you will find that this approach of gaining his attention can be continued by giving him freedom on the lead, and if your earlier training has been properly carried out he will be watching and waiting for the recall. Do not disappoint him, but when you call him in to you, have him walking at your left side for some five to ten seconds. Remember to use plenty of encouragement and praise. Do not bother about corners, about-turns, or a sit to finish, just have him happily walking at your side. The temptation of titbits can be a help, but you do not want him jumping all over the place. When you can keep his attention in this manner for some ten to fifteen seconds you are ready to break in more of the heel work elements.

To walk for some ten to fifteen seconds without any turns requires a fair bit of space. If this amount of ground is not readily available it will be necessary to put in at least one turn. Right turns only should be considered at this stage, as this fits in with previous training, where you tend to move away from your dog and you are in a position to draw him in. A left turn at this stage could mean bumping into him, and you wish to keep it as simple and easy as possible. Until now you should not have required to use the 'Heel' instruction during the heel work training – it has all been encouragement and praise to keep him by your side. If your build-up has been satisfactory there should be no need to use the instruction while walking in a straight line.

Now start making use of right turns to give you a square. Again, start from a free position and not the sit. As you are going into a right-hand turn, break off your encouragement to give the instruction to 'Heel', turn and continue with full encouragement and praise. In Element 3 of the recall you had already made use of this instruction, and you have made him sit at the heel position. That being so, it should not be difficult to introduce the sit to finish with a nice straight sit to heel.

As you are setting a foundation for a nice smart round of the heel on lead and heel free exercises you must walk smartly and expect the same from your dog. If you wait for him he will just slow down still further. Do not give him cause to heel at a sluggish pace. You want him to walk smartly, with his head in line with your left knee.

When he is walking nicely, with good right turns, introduce him to right about-turns. We wish to avoid left turns at the moment so it will be necessary to give an about-turn and then another to maintain the subsequent right turns. If you have plenty of room to work out of doors you can give alternate about and right turns as you wish. On the about-turn it is important that you do not wait for your dog. Get him to come round nice and close and smart.

At this stage you can also introduce the proper start to heel work. With the dog sitting by your left knee, build up some enthusiasm to go – you may find that he will require to be physically restrained whilst you build him up for the off. On the instruction 'Heel' step off with your left foot and give all the encouragement that is necessary. If you have to use the instruction to heel at any time other than starting off or immediately prior to a corner or about-turn you are not working on a good sound foundation. Remember to keep those training sessions short so that you can give and achieve hundred per cent attention.

The left turn can now be introduced. As your dog will not

be expecting it he will require to be conditioned for this change in his normal routine. The manoeuvre may best be accomplished by stopping and at the same time pulling back on the lead to prevent your dog from going ahead whilst you turn. At the same time give the instruction 'In' whilst you turn and then move off smartly with the instruction to heel, then give plenty of encouragement. The word 'In' will soon let him know that you are going to turn left and this turn can then become a continuous movement in the heelwork exercises. As long as you keep the sessions short and do not let inattention or boredom creep into your own or the dog's attitude, the instructions to heel will eventually be minimised to the instruction to start the exercise.

The need for encouragement during the exercise should now be reduced to take-off and turns and followed by a little praise. When this is accomplished with complete satisfaction the lead can be taken off for a very short spell with only right turns to concentrate on. While carrying out most of the training on lead, the off-lead work is built up slowly in the same manner as initially with the lead on, but return to plenty of encouragement and praise.

For trials work the dog will probably be required to carry out some of the heel work in a figure of eight. This can be round two posts about six feet apart or two people the same distance apart; it may also be carried out at a fast or slow pace.

Heel work at a fast pace will make a happy worker excited, and we shall hope you have achieved this. The excited dog requires little encouragement but should be kept under control. Basic training for fast pace is, of course, carried out on the lead where control can instantly be applied as the situation warrants.

The slow pace for heel work brings out a completely different situation. By the nature of the exercise your dog becomes very subdued, with time to let his mind wander on to other things. This must not be allowed – you must keep his attention the whole time. As you are asking so much in the way of attention, you should keep the slow heel work very short and build up the length of slow work very gradually.

There should never be any need to spend any more time on heel work than twice that required for a Class C competitive round. If any session is longer than that, more is liable to be lost than gained. You may have a dog doing excellent heel work a bit earlier by longer sessions but the inhibiting factor can reduce the effectiveness of training for the more independent exercises.

Temperament Test

As this is a test and not an exercise, training should not be necessary. In fact, training a dog of unsound temperament to stand up to this test would be against the principal objective of the test.

The least that is expected of a dog is to stand his ground whilst the judge approaches from the front then runs his hand over the dog's back. A dog that will not accept this certainly requires help to lead a less apprehensive life in the outside world, and that concerns me more than being trained to stand up to a temperament test. Almost any dog can be trained to stand firm and accept the approach of strangers, but this does not make him at ease in their presence. A dog who normally reacts with uncertainty needs to be conditioned into a more friendly state of mind to accept the world at large. That means introducing him into varying situations that will help in the long run. He requires gradual mixing – to be taken shopping, and to the local training club, where he will get the opportunity to meet people with other dogs. He should not be protected against the outside world, but at the same time he should not be forced into situations he is not ready for.

One conditioning method that can be of great help is the giving of titbits, especially when the dog is hungry. Always carry titbits with you, then when you meet somebody the dog is uncertain about give them some titbits so that they can entice

78

your dog to them. Let them feel your dog and make real friends. This approach can easily be extended to the training club, where 'doggy' people are more understanding. You can make use of a small number of people, say the same four or five until your dog has more than accepted them, he is looking for them and going forward to meet them as they approach. When they can approach your dog individually and stroke him at will without the use of titbits you are ready to extend his circle of friends. Add a couple of new ones and start afresh with the titbits. Remember this is more effective with a hungry dog than with a dog that is fed before going to the training club. As this friendliness through titbits will only be taking place during your presence you are in a position to give backing or support to your dog, and this will not affect his guarding instincts in the car or at home.

The approach suggested is not a means of beating the temperament test but one of making your dog more socially acceptable and thereby conditioned to the outside environment. He will, however, be suitably at ease and in a state of mind in which the temperament test will not have any effect on him. He will also be temperamentally conditioned to enjoy fully an obedience showing career.

I have judged dogs that have been 'trained' to withstand a temperament test, but these dogs were not conditioned to be socially acceptable animals. The trainers of these dogs are making a complete farce of the test and the reason for its introduction. I have certainly no intention of describing the training method that would achieve this kind of result.

The Stay Exercises – Sit, Down and Stand

The basic requirement for each of the stay exercises is the same: that the dog should remain in the position instructed and should not move, even on return of the handler, until the judge has indicated that the exercise is finished.

Each of the stay exercises is trained in the same manner,

although the final duration of the stay differs with each position. The sit-stay calls for two minutes in that position with the handler out of sight, the down requires ten minutes with handler out of sight, and the stand only requires one minute duration with the handler remaining in sight, although he will normally be required to turn his back towards the dog.

Although the stay exercises are very important in themselves, they are also the foundation of many other exercises, such as the agility, advance stand, sit and down, distance control and the send away. Handlers who intend channelling their activities into obedience competitions are advised to study the distance control exercises to ensure that they obtain the sit and down positions in a manner that will save retraining for distance control.

With all the stay exercises it is very important that the dog is never allowed to break a stay, either by coming out or by changing his position. Hidings or tellings-off after the event are of little or no value. Anticipation and prevention on the part of the handler will do a lot more good. A handler can only anticipate movement if he gives total attention to his dog during training for the stays. It is quite common to see handlers at a training club treating the stay exercise as an opportunity to have a good old chat. Then when they are told by the trainer that the dog has moved they tend to take it out on the dog for not obeying the instruction to stay. This, unfortunately, is a very common sight.

Sit-stay: The basic training for this exercise is already given in the foundation section. It is now necessary to build up to two minutes with the handler in sight. It is a good idea to extend the time in training to three minutes to create a more stable situation. To ask a dog to sit perfectly still for a long period is not very fair and quite unnecessary.

Whilst still at the stage of staying in sight, get some member of the family or friend of the dog to entice the dog gently to get up. He should not use the dog's name or a command but use a sensible approach to tempt your dog to relax from the exercise in hand. At the same time you must tell your dog to stay sitting where he is and make sure that he does not move. During the use of deliberate distractions your dog must not be allowed to move and you must be in a position to ensure that he knows you will note and prevent any tendency to move. When you are certain of your dog's ability to stay you can now move out of sight, by which we mean that you are out of his sight, not he out of your sight. Whilst out of sight you can occasionally speak to him to let him know you have not left him. Build up trust, give him full faith in you. He must understand that you will always return to him. As described in the foundation section, always use the same instruction, and the one most suited is 'Sit-stay'. The stay should mean to him that you will be back for him. If distractions are used when you are out of sight make sure that you are in a position to see exactly what is going on, then anticipate any move and get in quick with your voice to prevent it.

Down stay: The procedure for the down is identical to that of the sit, but this time you want your dog completely relaxed – he can go to sleep if he wishes. If you want him to stay for ten, fifteen or twenty minutes he must be completely relaxed and again have great faith in your return. Dogs move from the set stay positions for one of three main reasons. They may be:

1   Worried and concerned about something.
2   Bored with the whole procedure.
3   Just not understanding the requirements.

Any of these reasons can probably be attributed to the handler's approach and can only be corrected by him giving full consideration to his own general attitude and modifying it to establish a more suitable pattern.

Stand stay: It is very unnatural to ask a dog to stand still for one minute. Admittedly you are not asked to go out of sight. Again this exercise is trained in precisely the same manner as the 'sit' and 'down' stay. When you have reached the stage of turning your back on your dog you should still be in a position to watch him for any sign of movement. When you turn your head to watch him he will know and probably stand still, but he may soon learn to make a move when you are not looking. This is easily overcome by the use of a mirror, as you can then keep him in full view the whole time your back is turned towards him.

All stay exercises: When attending obedience shows and watching handlers give the final command before leaving their dogs in the stay exercises, I sometimes get the impression that most of the dogs must be deaf. Practically every handler seems to shout at the top of his voice commanding the dog to stay. If he is deaf he cannot hear you, if he is not deaf, why shout? If you train for obedience shows or working trials please try and break away from the traditional approach of shouting at the dog who is sitting, standing or lying by your side. It is quite unnecessary.

Class 'A' Recall

This exercise takes place with the dog being left at the sit or down (handler's choice) whilst the handler walks forward. He then calls his dog in to heel whilst he continues to walk forward, then halts with the dog sitting at his left side. The recall as given is also the finish for the send away exercise in Obedience Class 'B' and 'C'.

The 'A' recall must be considered as the easiest exercise to teach in the obedience repertoire provided that it is based on good and happy novice recall and good heel work, as it is really just a combination of both exercises.

However, the easiest way of breaking in the exercise without inhibiting the dog with the stay is to make use of a free recall whilst out for a walk. Call him in with great excitement and encouragement, use a hand signal to slap your side, and see that you are walking away from him as he comes running in. As soon as he reaches your side maintain the control through a dozen or so paces of heel work, halt with the sit as normal and then release him for fun and games. If you carry this out once only during your daily walk it will be surprising how quickly the main part of the 'A' recall has been accomplished.

All that is left to complete the training is to leave the dog at the sit, or down if preferred, walk away with the instruction to wait as with the novice recall, then call him in as before. In the early stages of this final part of training it may well be necessary to turn your head to give him all the encouragement necessary to get him to break the stay.

This is a simple exercise simply trained with the minimum of 'obedience' training.

Advanced Retrieve

By this we mean the retrieving of any article of reasonable proportions and composition, and it is remarkable what a dog can retrieve if he has the will to carry. I have had one dog retrieve a bucket full of water, and also a raw egg. I have had great fun with my dogs trying to retrieve an old motor tyre. I did not expect them to retrieve the tyre, and did not make them, but every time we found an old tyre on the beach my dogs have all enjoyed trying to bring it back to me. I think it gets a lot of frustration out of the system, and they would get most annoyed if I walked away and left them still trying to retrieve it.

The training for advanced retrieving should be a time for relaxed enjoyment, when the dog should be encouraged to pick up any article thrown or even kicked. I just have to kick an empty beer can and the first dog there picks it up. Start it all as fun and games and then on the odd occasion carry out the recall whilst he is running free with the article in his mouth. A good solid recall is, of course, necessary. When you do call him in he must respond as you would expect with the obedience retrieve. After finishing give him his article back and let him continue with his fun and games. He will soon learn the difference between fun and the need for an immediate and proper response to your instructions. Restrict this strict controlled recall with an article to possibly two occasions on one outing. During these fun sessions one full obedience retrieve should be included, with particular attention to prevent anticipation. If anticipation does occur repeat the exercise with firmer control and then get back to fun and games.

It would be impossible to go through all the types of articles one could expect to get in obedience or trials, but I have found that a motorcar sparking plug, being very heavy for its size, can cause problems, while a rubber balloon, not blown up of course, is very light and at times a dog wonders if he has anything in his mouth. Care should be taken to ensure that nothing is used that will be injurious to the dog.

If your foundation training is up to scratch, any attempt to mouth or chew articles can easily be stopped by the strength of your voice. He may chew whilst he is playing but as soon as you command his attention for a recall then the chewing must stop immediately until he is released from the controlled position.

With this approach to advance retrieving your dog will respond to any article an obedience or working trials judge cares to use.

Distance Control

In the words of the regulations (S2) the distance control exercise requires the following:

'The dog to Sit, Stand and Down at a marked place not less than ten paces from the handler, in any order on command from judge to handler. Six instructions to be given in the same order for each dog. Excessive movement, i.e. more than the length of the dog, in any direction by the dog, having regard for its size, will be penalised. The dog shall start the exercise with its front feet behind a designated point. No penalty for excessive movement in a forward direction shall be imposed until the back legs of the dog pass the designated point.'

Distance control is a very unnatural exercise to teach a dog and is probably the least purposeful exercise in the complete obedience routine. Its only value would appear to be to show the amount of precise control that can be achieved at a distance. The working distance is, however, very limited and is controlled by the size of the ring at obedience shows. When there are so many opportunities to exploit the natural inherited instincts of a dog it sometimes seems a pity to spend time on circus-type performances, but there are many people who disagree with this view judging by the number of Class C obedience competitors there are around.

With this exercise we must firstly consider how to make it seem natural to the dog and have him enjoy it. If we watch the antics at training classes and also listen to the 'shouting' of commands at obedience shows it is obvious that most dogs do not enjoy this exercise and their joy on completion shows in their obvious relief when it is all over. It is treated by most trainers and handlers as a completely submissive exercise, one that requires an overbearing approach where the commands are given in a manner of 'Thou must – or else.'

It is quite easy to train a dog in a natural manner to sit, stand or down, but quite another matter to obtain the main objective of the exercise.

The important and unnatural part of the exercise is the restriction in forward movement, and it is this restriction of movement by the dog that seems to bring out the worst in many handlers.

To obtain this basic requirement we should forget about the commitment to prevent the front feet from passing the designated point and concentrate our efforts on maintaining the original position of the dog's rear feet. If we can maintain the position of the rear of the dog throughout the six positional changes there can be no danger of the front feet moving beyond the designated point on completion of the sixth positional change. If the judge uses all possible changes in position during the six changes the dog will always finish back in the starting position – i.e. start at sit will finish at sit.

The training about to be described is centred on the sit position, moving into and out of the sit. The method of obtaining these changes in position should be trained as a way of life and become second nature to the dog. If you are contemplating training for Class C obedience then the approach of achieving the sit, stand or down should start at the training for the stays. When positioning the dog for the sit-stay the method should be applied which will achieve the movement required in taking up the position for distance control.

As the dog's area of contact with the ground in the sit position is approximately half that of the down or stand, it is obvious that foot movement is essential to move from the down or stand to the sit position. The most natural method for a dog to employ of his own volition is to draw his haunches towards his front feet as he sits, and then in standing up he will step forward into the stand; this movement alone will cost half a body length. Training should commence using the sit and the main position with movements to the stand and back to the sit, and also down and back to the sit. These position changes should be perfected before advancing to the next stage. The stand to down and reversed should be left until the other positions are being carried out with immediate response when you are standing no further than about three feet in front of the dog.

Stand-Sit-Stand: The purpose behind this is to get the dog to move his front feet back as he sits on his haunches, and this can be achieved by standing in front of him with your hand under his chin, stepping into him to assist him gently back into the sit position. Whilst you are doing this tell him to sit and lavish praise on him once it is accomplished. A titbit the instant he sits can be quite a booster and will help to reinforce your praise. Give him ten to fifteen seconds in this position whilst you stroke and praise him. You want your dog completely relaxed and not worried about being pushed into a submissive position. To change back to the stand change your own position and stand at the side of him and draw him back up into the stand position, if necessary putting your hand under his stomach to help him. There is every possibility that he will not like this approach, so care must be taken not to make it any more unpleasant than necessary. His front feet will have moved forward into the original stand position, and any slight backward movement of his hind legs can be ignored. Again, when implementing this change of position tell him to stand and give plenty of praise on completion of the positional change. However, do not let him step forward during this praise: a titbit may well be in order, but again beware of forward movement in his desire to obtain the titbit. In the early stages always keep him in the changed position for ten to fifteen seconds with praise and comforting before moving into the next position. Remember that those movements are all being carried out in an unnatural manner to the dog, and he should be made perfectly at ease between each stage. Repeat the full process three or four times before going on to some other part of your training programme.

Sit-Down-Sit: It should not be difficult to get a dog to go down from the sit position, since nothing unnatural is being asked of him and he just has to let his front feet slide forward. With a little encouragement and the aid of a titbit to entice him there should not be a problem, although care should be taken to ensure that he does not edge forward. However, I have found that the quickest drops into the down position have been gained by a more forceful method. If I try to demonstrate this method with one of my own trained dogs, he goes into the down himself before I get the chance to demonstrate the technique in full.

I have the dog sitting at my left-hand side and then I kneel beside him. I then put my left arm over his shoulder and my left hand behind his left pastern, at the same time putting my right hand behind his right pastern. As I give the word 'Down' I push both front feet from underneath him and at the same time let my own body go so that I fall on to my left elbow and thigh. I am in a position to keep him there and make a great joke of it, but if necessary I can come in with a hard and positive command to 'Stay down' then immediately give him praise and again make a joke of it. With this method a dog can learn very fast and still enjoy the result of the sudden movement. If the ground or floor is dirty that is how you will finish up, but a little dirt should not be considered a problem when the end result is so effective. Again in this positional change the rear of the dog stays in the same place and the front feet move forward.

To go from the down to the sit a titbit can be the best enticement. This time you are standing in front of your dog pressing forward with the instruction to sit whilst he is drawn up by the titbit. Without a titbit it will require your hand under his chin to help him back into the sit position.

The four positional changes already described take a bit of time to develop and training should continue until you can get instant response with each change from a distance of about three feet in front of the dog. When you are working from the front of the dog without any need to handle him you should have developed your own body and hand movements to reinforce the verbal instruction as to which position is required. In fact your movements will tell your dog what the next position will be and he can move into it before the verbal instruction is out. When all this becomes natural to him we can now consider training the stand to down and reverse.

Stand-Down-Stand: This positional change can now be tackled whilst standing in front of the dog. He is already accustomed to you standing about three feet in front of him, so you can try to maintain that distance as it gives him a good chance to assess your movements and anticipate the next change in position. At this stage you wish to take advantage of anticipation. Now put your dog into the stand and position yourself in front of him. Move as if you are to give the sit position and as he is moving into the sit position continue your movement and verbal instruction for the down. As he has been

88

well trained to go from the sit to down the continued movement should become automatic. From the down to stand a similar procedure should be adopted. Move forward as if to give the sit instruction and as he is moving into the sit position move back to draw him to stand, giving the verbal instruction at the same time. This approach makes the down-stand-down positional changes very easy and simple without any need for a demanding or overbearing attitude.

However, it is now necessary to consider the effect of the down-stand-down training on the stand-sit and down-sit positions. The dog has been conditioned to move right through from down to stand and from stand to down via the sit. When requesting the dog to go into the sit position from the down or stand it will now be necessary to instruct a 'Stay' as ne reaches the sit position to prevent a continuation of the movement.

Throughout the training of all the changes in the dog's position, your own physical movements have enticed and indicated the changes in position required. Your physical movements have been ahead of your verbal instructions which have acted as a reinforcement to these physical movements. Verbal instructions should now be timed to coincide with your physical movements.

The physical movement of enticement can now be minimised and then eliminated as an indication to the dog of the change of position. The verbal instruction will then become the motivation for the dog to change from one position to another.

Remember after each positional change to take the time and trouble to give him plenty of praise and let him know how clever he has been. Do not move more than three feet from him until complete perfection with immediate response is attained. Only then should you start increasing distance at a slow rate. Even with the increase in distance between yourself and the dog this distance should only be used on occasions with the bulk of the training to keep in trim being carried out at the distance of three to six feet in front of the dog.

The following diagrams will show the movements from the

starting line, or designated point, for each individual change of position (Figure 2), and also examples of the complete set of changes throughout the full exercise (Figure 3). The vertical base lines indicate the position of the dog's front feet at the start of the exercises. It will be noted that on occasions the front of the dog does go beyond the designated point but always comes back to the original position, so long as the hind legs are not permitted to move forward.

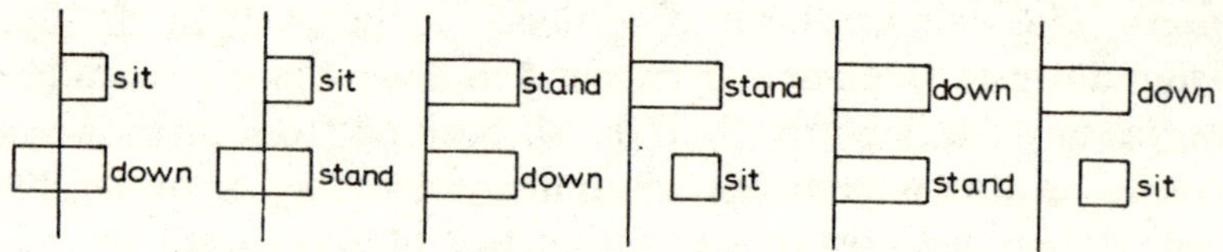

Fig. 2.   Distance control – the individual changes of position.

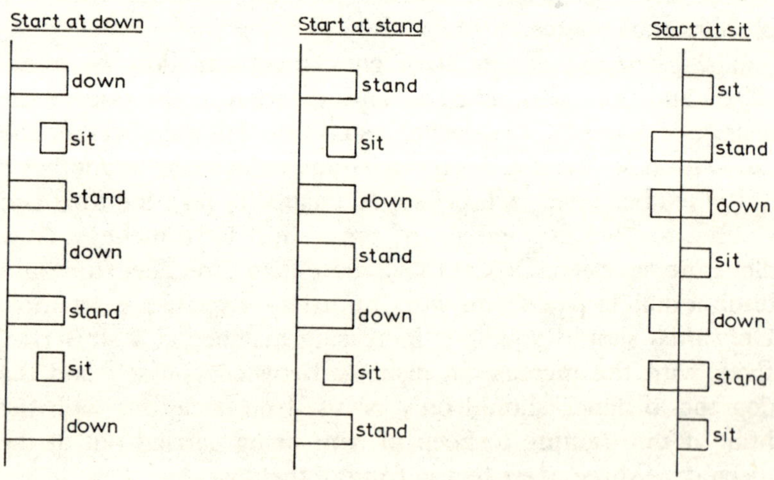

Fig. 3.   Distance control – the full exercise.

Advanced Stand, Sit and Down

Having trained for distance control and a good round of heel work, the introduction of this exercise to the obedience heel work should not be a problem, but again like all the other exercises an easy introduction is essential until the dog fully understands the routine.

During a heel on lead session, stop and indicate to your dog the position required, praise him, tell him to wait and walk away from him. You can either go round in a circle or turn and pass him, turn again and walk back to his side from behind him, stop, praise him, pick up the lead and walk forward with him at heel. Each time give him the instruction as you stop and ensure he goes immediately into that position before you leave him. When the pattern has been established drop the lead as you give the positional instruction and carry on walking, but look back to ensure he has carried out the instruction correctly and promptly. Do not bother about completing the circuit, go right back and tell him how good and clever he is. When you are quite satisfied with the results remove the lead and repeat the process but carry out the full routine by calling him to heel as you pass him. He will probably lack the understanding at first, so get him excited as you pass and give all the encouragement you can to take up the position at heel.

Send Away and Redirect

The send away can be rather a slow and tedious exercise to teach a dog, especially in working trials where anything up to 200 yards can be called for. When we add a redirection to the send away we must give very serious consideration to the approach which is going to create a happy and responsive dog. Many a dog will do a good fast long send away, but most of them are rather concerned about the 'size nines' thumping behind them like they do during training sessions; it is evident that some dogs are terrorised into performing this exercise. It must be fully appreciated that the send away and redirect are quite unnatural exercises for a dog to perform, and we should therefore convert them in training into an exercise with purpose, as once the habit is formed and consolidated the reason for wanting to go out can be put into the background and finally eliminated.

We shall treat the send away and redirect as two separate exercises and combine them when we are satisfied that both are to a standard where immediate and fast response is attained.

Although distance control training can assist in obtaining the control required at the end of the send away, working trials people do not normally train distance control exercises. We shall now consider this as an exercise that has no connection with any other exercise, although admittedly the down stay is a help. The main elements of the exercise are as follows:

1   Set the dog up and prepare him to go out in the correct direction.
2   Send him out to the spot required.
3   Stop him and put him down on the spot selected.

If we look at these elements we can see that there is not much use in setting him up if he does not know where to go, and if he did, there is less sense in sending him if we cannot control him when he gets there. The last element is therefore the crucial one, and the basis for training the complete exercise. The instant drop into the down position should have an incentive, and we must create the situation where the dog wants to drop whenever the instruction is given, no matter where he is or what he is doing.

Make use of an old jacket, cardigan, piece of canvas or a carpet square, so long as it is something you can cut up and make smaller at a later date. Teach your dog to go down on this article – we shall call it the square. I prefer to teach the dog to go down via the sit, as described in the distance control training.

92

The incentive for the send away now comes in, and this is that the real desire to go out fast and go down is for the reward of food. Initially the dog is on the lead and taken to the square and dropped. Immediately he 'hits the deck' you produce food and give him a titbit whilst in the down position. Call him up, walk round, then return to the square and drop him again, produce your little container of food and give him some more.

At the same time, of course, you are giving him plenty of praise for going down. When he knows that he must drop immediately he is at the square and he looks at you as much as to say 'Well, I'm waiting, where's the food?', you are ready to press on. Your food container should be of a type that he cannot open. He will by this time recognise the container every time it is produced. Now is the time to put the container on your square and let him see you do it. Again repeat the performance of walking round with him on the lead and then return to the square. Drop him, open the container and give him his usual titbit along with the praise. Continue with this procedure until he pulls you to the square and you will probably find he goes down without instructions. This does not mean that you can leave them out. Always give him the 'Down' instruction as he is dropping.

You will find that he learns pretty quickly at this stage and a foundation is being built up on something he wants to do. To carry out this training after a dog has been fed for the day will probably have limited success, but to base this procedure on a hungry dog can be very effective. We shall assume that all training is being carried out prior to the main meal of the day.

Still working on the lead with the dog pulling you to the square every time, you now have the basis for a send away, so every time he moves towards the square you give a gentle instruction to go. He is going anyway and does not require an instruction, but this is the build-up for the instruction that will be necessary at a later date. This is the conditioning process in action. The desire for food is strong and he knows that he must drop on the square before he receives it. When you are completely satisfied that his desire is strong you can then take him the usual distance from the square – this should be somewhere between five and ten paces away – slip the lead and let him go. Again as he is going use the 'Go' instruction, and the 'Down' as he reaches the square. Follow up and give him his titbit out of the container. Do not overdo any single session, but stop whilst he is still hungry and keen.

It will now be appreciated that we have conditioned the dog to wish to go at speed to the place of our choice and immediately go down on that spot. When this has been fully achieved with a great desire to be released to get there we can consider training the send away as an exercise. We therefore continue to put out our square with the container of food on it and continue as before, but instead of releasing him make him sit for a few seconds facing the direction of the square and build up for the release, which you accompany with the encouragement to 'Go'. At this stage accept his impatience, as you have been building this up and creating it. You can now make further use of the loop of cord attached to the slip chain, as with the foundation retrieve. It is important to maintain this desire to get out there: you are physically restraining him, at the same time gently encouraging him and building up for the release.

Your distance at this stage will probably be no more than twenty yards, and his square with container will be in full view. Each time you make him sit before releasing him he is positioned to face directly at his square. You are therefore conditioning him to go straight out in the direction he has been facing. It is important that each time you send him out, although you can stand still until he is down, you always go out to him and give him his titbit out of the container. Distance can now be increased gradually up to about fifty yards. To do this, always start with a short send away then move back a little and send him out to the same spot. Do not become too ambitious, and if you find that you have expected too much go back a stage to consolidate.

If you have the ground try the round-the-clock approach with your square in the centre. This will get him used to the changing background of his send away square.

Now is the time to prepare for the day when the food container will not be left on the square. You can put the container under a corner of the square but let him see you do this, so that he knows it is to be there when he arrives. When he is accustomed to this and does not expect to see it you can then keep it in your pocket and only take it out to give him his titbit as usual when he is down on the square. It is important that you go out to him every time with his titbit. If you are asking him to go back and forward in training, the least you can do is cover the same distance. If you find it physically tiring, he probably finds it mentally tiring too. It is therefore time to stop the session.

You can now start reducing the size of your square so that it is not readily seen, and gradually increase your distance still further. The stage will now be reached when he cannot see the square whilst sitting at your side and it is only the knowledge that the square has always been straight out which will take him straight out.

Just as the dog's keen anticipation was your greatest ally in training him to retrieve, it is again the strongest force behind the send away. Now it requires to be curbed, and he must understand that he should wait until you verbally release him. This will take time, but be patient: you have created a situation where he has now to be restrained.

Two things can now be done to prepare for the send away without the square:

1 After a few send aways to the square pick it up then send him to the same spot and drop him where the square has been. You can finish by putting it back for the last send away of the session.
2 You can also try dropping him about fifty yards out and

before he reaches the square. If this is not initially successful do not persist until the first approach has been successfully carried out a few times.

Eventually you will be able to reduce the square to a size that will make it practical to do away with it. Remember that it is a long-term training exercise and do not rush it. Until this exercise has been perfected remember to go out to him every time and reward him. Any laziness on your part will slow down the progress or reduce the reliability of his performance. When you are walking out to him let him know how good he has been. It is far better to let him know you are pleased than have him in doubt as you are walking out.

Do not on any account try to correct a wrong direction when training the send away by redirecting. This will achieve nothing and will tend to confuse the dog. It is also a sure sign that the training is not being consolidated at each stage.

The send away for obedience shows can be relatively short. I doubt if they are over twenty yards, although great accuracy is required. I remember taking Callum, after gaining all his working titles, into obedience at Class A and B levels. He did a beautiful send away until he saw all the huge marker cones for the square, when he immediately veered off and I lost a barrowload of points. A couple of shows later he won his first obedience prize – first in Class B. The motto being, if you are going to compete in obedience, train for the conditions you can expect.

Redirection: Although redirection is only a correcting factor which could save a few points in the obedience ring, it is an important part of directional control in working trials. The training principle is identical to that for the send away.

When you have reached the stage in the send away of reducing your square, cut it in two equal parts – you then have two squares to be used as 'bases'. By the time you have reached this stage in the send away you can consider training for redirection.

Training for redirection must not come at the end of the

A training club scene showing an early stage in the training of the sit-stay exercise where the handlers are in a position of control.

Training club agility tuition–an intermediate phase in training for the scale jump.

Puppy Fraser socialising with house pet Dornie and police dog Bob.

Ardfern Bruar, Ardfern Barry and Ardfern Brora at seven weeks old

Preparation for
the recall
exercise. Kusa
being given the
instruction to wait.

Handler leaving
Kusa in the sit
position.

Below: Handler
in position with
Kusa waiting to
be recalled.

A prompt response to the recall.

Below left: Kusa sits in front of her handler and awaits the final instruction to heel.

Below right: Kusa going round to heel to complete the recall exercise.

Honey at an elementary stage of training for the scale jump.

Honey being introduced to the long jump.

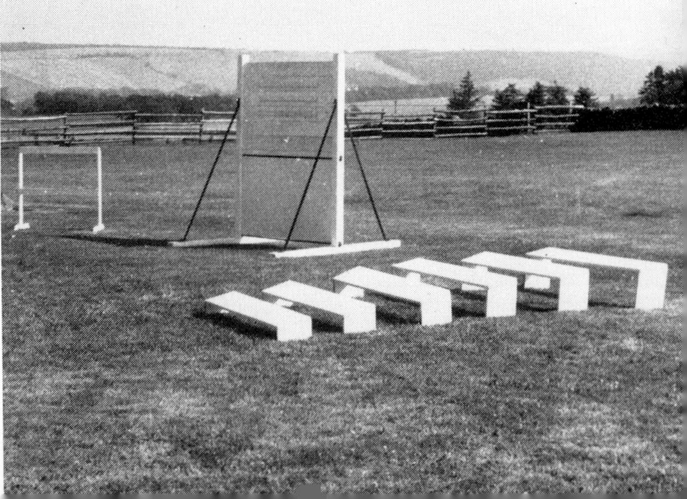

Equipment set out for the agility tests.

Police dog Cito clears the long jump. (Reproduced by permission of the *People's Journal*, Dundee.)

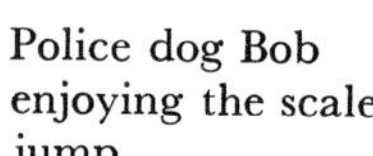

Police dog Bob enjoying the scale jump. . .

. . . and taking the clear jump

Above: Fitting a harness in preparation for tracking.

The start of the track–Kusa shows her eagerness as she picks up the scent.

Below: Kusa´ takes the first 'corner' and indicates the new direction of the track.

Kusa finds the article left by the track layer.

Kusa's handler shows her appreciation with praise on completion of a good track.

send away in training. The send away and redirection must not be put together until each has been perfected separately. Consider them to be two completely separate exercises until you are satisfied with each one.

Place both your squares about three to five yards apart, put your dog down on one and give him his titbit, then take your food container and place it on the other square. Go back to your dog and release him from the down to go over to the other square, so that he drops for his titbit. Repeat back and forwards a few times. You are conditioning him to go from the down on a short send away to the other square. You can now stand in front of the unoccupied square and release him from the other and as he is going over encourage him then give him the 'Down' as he drops. Each time you let him go from left to right give the full-stretched arm signal with the instruction 'Right'. Repeat the process from right to left giving the instruction 'Left', but each time use the food container as the inducement.

As with the send away, hide the food container for a spell and then remove it completely. Gradually increase distance between squares, and between yourself and the squares. Remember with every redirection you must go up to your dog, praise him, recognise that the titbit induced him to go and give him the titbit as a reward.

When you can move back fifty yards or more and have him redirecting for fifty yards or more you can then think of combining it with an equally good send away. Do not expect a perfect combination right away. Put out both squares, send him to one, give him his praise and titbit, and then redirect from a reasonably close position, something he has done before and understands.

When this procedure has been fully established carry out the full send away, move part of the way towards him and then redirect. Do not do this at the start of a training session but break him in gently.

What total distances should you train for? That is up to yourself, but in trials it is unusual to get more than a 200 yard send away with a 100-yard redirect, and 100 yards and 50 yards respectively are more common.

There are no quick methods of training the send away or redirect but there are plenty of unreliable methods. We can see the result of them at any working trial or obedience show. One last word on titbits: dry biscuits can be rather uninteresting and not much of an inducement to do something that is quite unnatural, but a nice juicy piece of meat or tripe can be quite an inducement to make his actions very natural.

Speak and Cease Speaking on Command

Who needs to teach a normal and healthy dog to speak? It is the most natural activity for a dog to give voice, and yet we can have so much trouble getting a dog to speak when we want him to. It is reasonable to say that one dog takes more easily to 'speak on command' than another, but I think that most of our problems in teaching 'on command' are caused by our own failings. One of these is the very use of the phrase 'speak on command' – if we try to teach a dog by commands we are on a loser right away. There are only two ways that I know of to teach a dog to speak when required, and they are:

1 By encouragement when he starts of his own accord.
2 By inducing him to speak by creating the situation where he will want to speak.

Both methods can be used together, but it depends a great deal on his upbringing whether the second approach is worth pursuing during the early stages. Firstly, we should recognise that we cannot 'command' a dog to speak until he has been fully trained, and even then it is doubtful if the use of commands would meet with much success. We can, however, ask, request or induce a trained dog to speak when we desire it.

Our main problems are caused by telling an untrained dog in this exercise to be quiet every time he feels he has some reason to bark. He becomes inhibited, and when the time comes for

98

you to want him to speak he is so inhibited that it becomes impossible to induce him to speak when required. I made a mistake of this nature with one bitch. The older dog in the house had been taught to speak when required, and if he had reason to bark of his own accord, say somebody coming to the door, there was no problem in telling him to 'shut up'. However, the young bitch, who did not bark very much anyway, obviously took this to mean her as well. She was inhibited from the start. Admittedly I left it a bit late, but when I decided to start getting her to speak I would make use of a visitor to the house, the postman, milk boy, anybody, and when she barked I would encourage her. Initially, as soon as I said anything, even with the greatest of encouragement, she would immediately go quiet. For too long she had been conditioned to stop as soon as she heard me tell the old fellow to be quiet. It took a great deal of gentle encouragement to get her to continue barking when she started on her own. It proved to be a long hard slog to get over the problem I had created with a bitch that should have been helped from the start and not hindered.

If we now look at the working trials exercise we see that not only are we being asked to get the dog to speak but we are also required to make him stop when required. We may be required to get him to speak again and then stop again. As with all other exercises we break the exercise into elements and work through each stage.

Initially we make use of voluntary speaking and encourage him for a few seconds only, then distract him from the cause. The words you use are less important than the way you use them. The phrase used, however, should include the main word or two words that you wish to use finally, and as training develops the main words are emphasised to create the main inducement. As time goes on you will be able to use the main word or words on their own. Hand signals can also be developed if you wish – in fact they can be of great assistance as an inducement – but if you are also training for obedience competitions be careful not to use hand signals that can be confused with distance control instructions.

In the early stages go up to your dog when you encourage him to speak, because you do not want him to come to you.. The value of this will be realised when you start training him to speak at a distance and he must stay there.

When you feel that he has progressed sufficiently encourage him to think there is cause to speak, for instance somebody coming up to the door. Do not play on that one too often, he may well get wise to it. Praise him from the start and always let him know how pleased you are with him – again titbits can be a help. Inciting him to speak for his supper can be of great assistance. Holding a piece of meat in a clenched fist can also be very useful, so long as he knows it is there. When it comes to competing he does not need to know it is not there. The objective is conditioning and forming the desired habit or response to your verbal or physical incitement. A satisfactory speak is only of value if you can stop it. This may require a two-second overbearing outburst of 'Enough' from yourself, two seconds of shock treatment, and this must be made effective, but immediately incite him to start again and then the same to stop again. The successful application of this approach can lead on to a slightly longer delay between stopping and restarting.

Achieving distance between yourself and your dog should not be any problem, but if it is, hook him on to a fence and get him used to speaking from a distance. Use the same spot until he makes no attempt to strain on the lead, then leave him at the same spot with the lead attached to his slip collar but with the other end loose. Let him believe he is attached. When you are satisfied that he is going to make no attempt to come forward try with the lead off. If there is any attempt at any time to come forward hook him to the fence again and consolidate through each stage.

The next move is to use a new spot and assess his reaction when tied. From then on use different places and without the fence behind him.

100

A dog who has been taught to speak and cease speaking is generally much easier to quieten than a dog that has not had the benefit of this training.

Steadiness to Gunshot

Like the temperament test in obedience this is not an exercise that requires training but a test to assess the dog's stability. Although no training should be necessary, in fact I think it would be very difficult to train a dog to stand up to close gunshot. However, most dogs may well require to be conditioned to accept and ignore the noise of a gun. It is, of course, quite acceptable if the dog just turns to note the origin of the noise.

No dog should be initiated to the gun from close up. His reaction must be tested from a distance. It is very useful to purchase a starting pistol: although the noise is not so great, especially at a distance, the crack is very sharp and is extremely effective from close up.

I have found the best approach to initiating the further conditioning for steadiness is to make use of the gun whilst out for a walk with the dog loose and enjoying himself. Wait until there is quite a distance between yourself and the dog and let the gun off once. Immediately call your dog in and run away from him as if you were having a game with him. The number of occasions you can do this depends entirely on his reactions. Once on the first outing may be enough. In fact if your dog is not happy at all you may only be able to do this once on each outing until it bothers him no more.

Remember that a dog who is frightened by a close-up shot may never get over it. This is one form of conditioning where it pays to be overcautious. During conditioning do not leave him at a stay whilst you fire the gun – you could ruin the stay exercises. And it is preferable, at this stage, not to let a friend fire the gun. You can control the timing and your own reactions better when you fire it yourself. It is also better to have the dog coming towards the noise than cringing away from it. When you can walk with the dog at your left side and fire the gun in your right hand you are ready for the 'steadiness to gunshot' test, and then somebody else can fire the gun for you.

Chapter Six

Agility Exercises

General

The agility exercises are generally confined to working trials and consist of three different types of jumps:

1 The scale jump – a scramble jump at six feet high and returning back over the jump.
2 The long jump – a low obstacle nine feet in length.
3 The clear jump – a plain framework to be cleared at three feet high.

A mature fit dog who has been trained properly will find these jumps easy to negotiate and a very enjoyable way of expending a build-up of energy. Some people seem to feel that the scale jump of six feet is asking too much of a dog, and one 'authority' has gone so far as to say that it is potentially dangerous and completely pointless and should be dropped from the set of tests. I can only say that people who think and talk this way do not know how to train correctly or fail to recognise the basic need for the dog to be mature and fit in order to carry out these exercises. We have the pleasure from time to time of watching the RAF Demonstration Team at work and it is great to see the enthusiasm these dogs have in negotiating eight feet or more on the scale. This shows the physical capabilities of our breed and also their mental approach when channelled in the correct direction. It should be noted, however, that the RAF do not allow their dogs to drop on the far side of the scale from these heights. They have a platform constructed to ensure that the drop is taken in two stages.

To jump a dog who is too young may well create permanent physical damage and to jump an unfit dog will create an additional strain on the system which can well have a damaging and lasting effect. Either of these conditions can also affect the dog's mental outlook on jumping, which would certainly have an effect on future training. This does not mean that we should not train a young dog or one being built up to full fitness for agility, but we should consider the degree of physical exertion required and the landing conditions in relation to his age and fitness.

It is difficult to lay down hard-and-fast rules relating the age of a dog to the heights or lengths to be covered, and there is no doubt that the scale requires special consideration. The effects of landing from the scale jump are much greater than the take-off. A young dog dropping from a height of six feet or so with his full weight being taken on his shoulders can do himself much more harm than with any other element in the agility tests. The training heights being applied are controlled to some degree by the size and construction of the dog – a lightly built animal will not hit the ground with the same force as a heavily built one. The ground conditions also play a big part – a good thick carpet of grass will probably give the best take-off and landing conditions. A nice soft bed of sand at one side may ensure a soft landing but it does not help a dog to react to more normal conditions and it is quite unsatisfactory for the return take-off. Indoor training with mats may be satisfactory for the earlier stages in training, but they should be avoided for the more advanced training unless special conditions have been thought out and carefully applied. As a rough guide I would feel that training to about $4\frac{1}{2}$ feet on the scale jump at the age of about fifteen months would be just about right. A dog properly conditioned and trained will scale the increase to six feet in two or three weeks. The grading of the long jump could be in the region of seven feet at the age of fifteen months with the increase to full length similar to the scale. The full clear jump can, however, be taken at about the fifteen months although there is no reason why all three jumps should not be progressed to the full requirements at the same time.

The basis for good keen jumping is undoubtedly that of conditioning, habit and fitness for the exercises. Never take the slightest chance of a dog being injured on any of the jumps. Training at a suitable pace, the handler's correct mental approach and common sense will prevent injuries. The amount of jumping a dog is asked to carry out must be regulated according to the stage in training. There may be no problem in taking a dog over the first stages in jumping for six or so jumps on each session but twice on each jump will be sufficient when the full requirements have been reached.

Scale Jump

The scale jump should be a vertical wall of wooden planks, at least three feet wide, and may have affixed on both sides three slats evenly distributed on the top half of the jump. It will be appreciated that this piece of equipment should be made of the best materials, well and sturdily built. It is required to take the full weight of the dog, with a good landing force as the dog hits the top of it. Figure 4 shows a typical construction of this jump.

The dog is required to scale, drop on the other side and stay in the stand, sit or down position (handler's choice) until instructed to return. He should then sit in front of the handler before returning to heel.

To facilitate training the wooden planks or boards should each be about six inches in depth with one board three inches deep. This allows for a gradual increase in height of three inches at a time. A dog conditioned to scale at a particular height will not notice the addition of a three-inch board but will certainly note the increase of six inches in height.

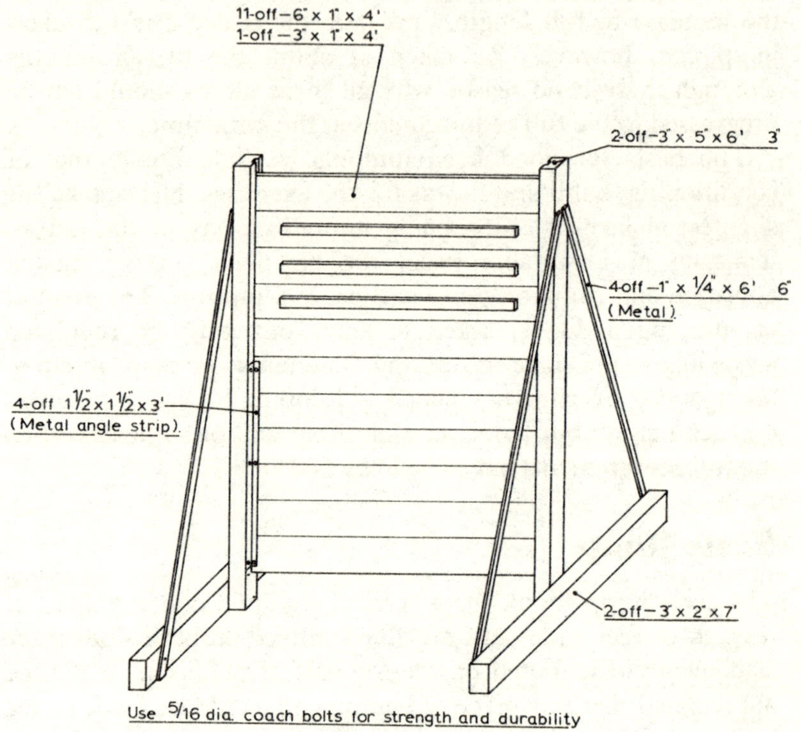

Fig. 4. Scale jump.

The full training procedure should be geared to obtaining the correct mental approach. This is an exercise that your dog should enjoy, and he certainly will not enjoy it if he is forced in any way. We therefore start with six to nine inches in height and our first conditioning process is that of going between the uprights and over this low board. This can be great fun as you, with the dog on the lead, run and take the jump with great excitement, returning with the same excitement. It is all a big game with about half a dozen repeats, the main objective being to stop before the dog gets fed up with the procedure. Each time you take this low jump with him you give the excited instruction 'Over' and on the return you use the instruction 'Back'. Full conditioning has taken place when he is ready to jump ahead of you and you can stop at the jump as he continues over while you give him all the encouragement that is necessary.

When this conditioning process is fully effective we now require to consider the next stage in training and the habits we are encouraging. It is important that we consider the stay at the far side of the jump and we must also consider the importance of maintaining enthusiasm by not inhibiting the dog. There is no doubt that forcing him to stay on the far side at this stage can be inhibiting, but on the other hand if we continue to encourage the immediate return we are building up for a condition of anticipation at a later stage. As a compromise we may well find that the continued build-up of enthusiasm is maintained until we have reached a height of two to three feet. We have increased the height by three inches at a time and allowed him to clear the jump giving the fullest possible encouragement to go over and immediately return. All this has been carried out on the lead.

Now is the time to create a positive delay with physical restraint, but verbally building up for the release. By standing about three feet back from the jump your dog will not be able to clear it but will use the pressure of front and rear feet on the top board to help himself over. Enthusiasm must be maintained, and the important thing at this stage is to teach him to use the correct scaling action, as this will help him achieve the full height of six feet when the time comes. Consolidate with this approach but at the same time make him sit at your side until you are ready to release him. Do not worry at this stage about his wanting to break the stay. Physically restrain him at the sit until you are ready to release him, then gradually reduce the distance between his sitting position and the jump until he is sitting relatively close to the boards. Remember the jump is still between two and three feet high and he is still on the lead.

Each time he touches the ground at the other side you immediately call him back, while you must move back yourself to allow him landing room. By moving close in for the jump over, you are creating the conditions that necessitate a scaling approach to jumping. As you increase the height you move back a little to maintain a similar scaling angle, reducing the dog's impression of additional height. In achieving and consolidating at a height of three to four feet let us consider just how far you have progressed:

1 The dog is still on the lead.
2 He will sit but probably requires to be restrained until physically released to take the jump.
3 He is jumping from a distance that will create the necessary scaling action.
4 On landing at the other side he returns immediately with a scaling action, while you are moving back to give him landing room.
5 You have an eager dog scaling a height of three to four feet.
6 He is responding to your instructions 'Over' and 'Back'.

It is now advisable to achieve the full requirements of the jump at this height, and to consolidate, before even thinking about increasing the height.

Can you now take the lead off and know that he will automatically return without any hesitation? If not, you are not in a position to advance further in the training schedule and have probably moved too quickly through at least one of the stages. This should be rectified before progressing further.

We now assume that the lead can be taken off and the loop of cord can again be attached to the slip chain and used for any restraint that is required.

There are now three elements to be worked on before increasing the height of the jump:

1 Anticipation in going over the jump. You have already had to cure anticipation with the retrieve and probably the send away; the method is just the same. It is

preferable to condition for this sit to await the release to jump and consolidate on it before tackling the next step. Do not confuse the dog with too many changes in previously accepted routines.

2   A proper finish. On returning over the jump, the dog should sit in front of you and then go round to heel. Through the foundation training for the recall and retrieve he already knows exactly what is wanted, and it is just a case of conditioning him into this position at the finish of the jump.

(I put these two items first because the dog has already experienced them and should come into line with your requirements quickly. They should not take anything away from the enthusiasm you have been so patient in building up.)

3   The stay at the far side of the jump.

The question now is, how does one tackle Element 3, and do you use the stand, sit or down position? The answer is partially dependent on the dog's natural reactions. Why should a dog be forced or trained to sit if he prefers to stand or go down? There may well be good reasons for putting him into an 'unnatural' position. The stand tends to encourage a dog to wander, either away from the jumps or, if he is too keen, he can move right in to the base of the jump. Probably no problem at three feet high but quite a problem at six feet. The down position can require a much more forceful attitude on the part of the handler and may well draw too much from the enthusiasm you have been so careful to cultivate. The sit position is a compromise: it prevents the movement afforded by the stand and is generally more acceptable to the dog than the down. The sit also seems to be the most alert position. The position is your choice, derived from your knowledge of your own dog, but the training described here will be that required for the sit. As before, release the dog for the jump and as he is going over follow him to the jump and as soon as he lands on the far side tell him to stay. As you are standing hard against the jump his return is blocked and he is caught off balance (mentally). Speak gently to him and instruct him to stay. Ensure that he is steady, keep speaking to him and walk round beside him. Tell him how clever he is and put him into the sit position, return to the other side of the jump and keep chatting to him. When you are ready, move back from the jump and call him back to finish normally. Continue with this procedure until you feel that he will go into the sit as instructed when he lands on the other side of the jump. Again build up and consolidate until you have no need to move from the near side when you send him over.

On the completion of these elements the full exercise is being carried out at a height of three to four feet and it only requires the gradual build-up of three inches at a time until the full six feet is attained. Remember that each time the height is increased you may move back slightly with the dog to give him the full opportunity to scale properly. At the full six feet high you will be standing six to nine feet back from the jump.

Voice control and timing can be very critical in achieving a good jumper. An unnatural or harsh voice can put a dog off, and failure is also caused by the faulty timing of instructions to the dog. A handler should always give full consideration to these factors and not be too ready to blame the dog for what may well have been his own fault. Remember, do not overdo any training session.

Long Jump

The long jump is generally made of five or six boards individually supported at a slight angle so that the nine feet spread gives an impression, at dog-eye level, of one continuous board. Figure 5 gives a typical construction of this jump.

The dog is required to clear this jump and remain under control until rejoined by the handler, who may approach this jump with the dog or stand by the jump as he instructs the dog to advance and clear the boards. He must not, however, proceed beyond any part of the jump ahead of the dog.

The conditioning process is again the foundation of this

agility exercise. We start with the creation of great pleasure in clearing a single board along with the handler. As the conditioning should take place with a single board, and the smallest one at that, there may be no need to use the lead, but use it if you feel it to be necessary in the very early stages. If there is any need to use it beyond initial conditioning this

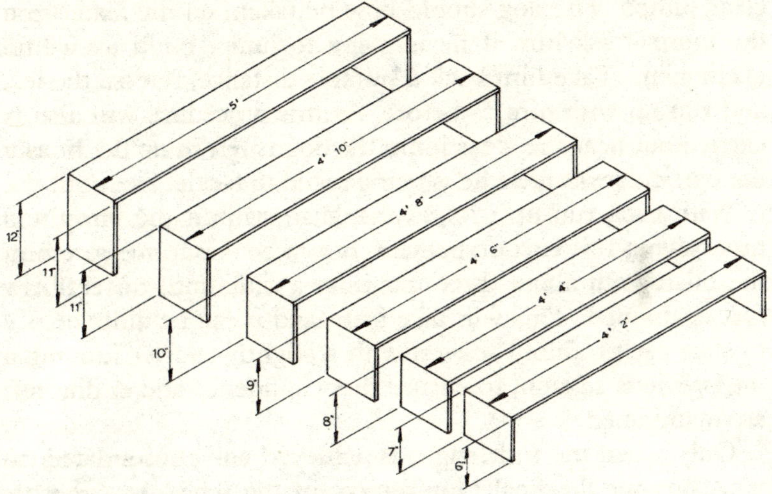

All wood to be 7" to 8" wide and 5/8" to 3/4" thick.
Boards to fit on top of each other to facilitate storage.

Fig. 5. Long jump.

indicates very strongly that the foundation has not been consolidated and training should be taken back to the relevant stage.

After the conditioning with one board a second board should be added close to the front one, the training to proceed until all the boards are in place close to each other. During this period each jump should be taken with the dog and handler running at a good pace. In the early stages the handler should clear the jump with the dog and later he can run past the jump as the dog clears it. Every jump requires full encouragement from the handler with the excited instruction to jump. The same instruction of 'Over' can be used as with the scale.

With the boards in position and close to each other, the total length will be about four feet. The dog should now be very eager and keen to take this jump. The conditioning can now be completed before the length is extended any further and in such a way as not to cause confusion in the dog's mind when he is asked to clear the long jump in the presence of the scale and clear jumps. The dog should now be taken, on the lead, up to the jump – ask him if he is going to jump, build up a little excitement. Take him back a suitable distance, release the lead and run up with him as before. As this procedure will also be carried out near the clear jump the dog is left in no doubt as to the particular obstacle he is being asked to tackle.

With each run up it is advisable to go past the jump with him, giving full encouragement as you go. Continue to extend the boards out about three inches at a time until the full nine feet is attained. This will take time, and it can be quite helpful to start each training session with a slightly shorter jump than the previous session, to ensure that confidence and enthusiasm are maintained.

Only when the full length is achieved and consolidated can you consider the final requirement of the schedule – that the handler must not proceed beyond any part of the jump ahead of the dog. The fact that you now stop at the jump should not have any effect on your dog, but you only require to stop occasionally to ensure that it does not affect him.

Voice control and timing can be critical and it is important that a handler can develop an approach which will be maintained in competitions. Again, remember not to overdo any training session.

Clear Jump

For training purposes, the three-foot clear jump should be constructed with a fixed top bar. Although the space below the bar may be left open it is preferable to have a strengthening bar more than half way down. A stabilising diagonal bar may also be required to give rigidity. Figure 6 gives a typical construction.

The dog is required to clear this jump and remain under control on the far side until rejoined by the handler. As with the long jump the clear jump is informal and does not require quite the strictness of control which is required for the scale. Having said that, it should still be recognised that control is required and that the exercise should finally be carried out in a smart and attractive manner.

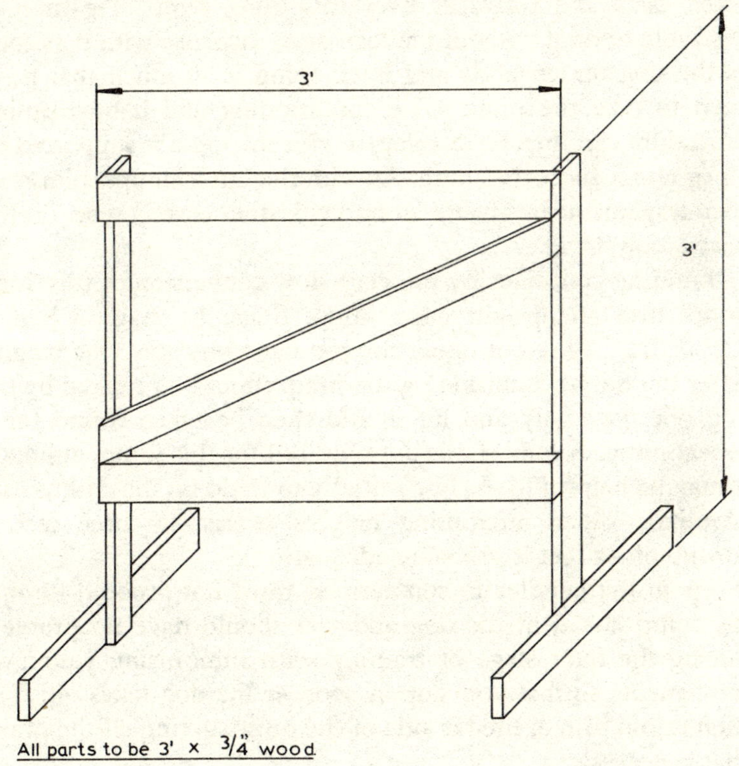

Fig. 6.   Clear jump.

The conditioning process, as with the scale and long, is the development of pleasure and fun to do something that is natural – and what is more natural than a dog jumping? Unfortunately there are many unnatural ways being used to train a dog to carry out a natural function. Any dog who has the physical ability and the driving desire can cope with any of these jumps if left to his own devices.

The start to conditioning for the clear jump is made by resting the jump with the top bar on the ground, at a right angle to the normal jumping position. The dog can then be taken back and forwards over this 'long jump'. Again it is desirable to do it without the lead or to dispense with it as soon as the dog understands and is enjoying it so much that he is keen to take the jump. The conditioning and habit-forming procedure can then be developed with the top bar supported by a peg about six inches high. As with the other jumps, plenty of encouragement is given, along with the correct use of the instruction 'Over'.

Training continues by the very slow conversion of this 'long jump' into an upright clear jump. Stage by stage a higher supporting peg is put under the top bar to increase the height. After the initial conditioning the jump should be cleared by the dog one way only and he should then be taken round for a repeat jump. A long run is not required for this jump, although it may be helpful to use one initially to build up the enthusiasm required. When attempting heights nearer to three feet, a run-up of six feet is probably adequate.

Again the handler in competition must not proceed beyond the jump ahead of the dog and you should have no problem during the later stage of training with minimising your own movements so that you stop as soon as the dog takes off. You then rejoin him at the far side of the jump, giving all the praise that is necessary.

Chapter Seven

Nosework Exercises

General

What can we teach a dog about nosework? Frankly, I do not think we can teach him a single thing. We can, however, assess the effects of his scenting and watch his reactions to certain conditions, and we can channel his actions and reactions to suit our own purposes so long as we have the knowledge and ability to interpret his thinking and make sound judgment of the strength of his inherited asset. As we cannot experience the scenting sensations of a dog we can only study his reactions and assess the conditions that have created them. We also have the invaluable experience built up by handlers before us.

We do not know how a dog can determine the difference in scent between one person and another, nor do we know how he can determine the direction of a track just by checking a few footsteps. There are theories on how a dog can make those determinations and also on differing ground conditions, and some of these guesses are probably near the mark – but which? It is a fact, however, that a dog can tell the difference in scent from one person to another, and that he can tell the direction of a track and the difference in time scale from one scented track to another. I therefore feel that we should forget about training a dog to use his nose, for if we attempt to train him to do something he knows so much better than any human being, we can add confusion and domineering control where absolute confidence should reign.

A dog can be conditioned to react to our guidance, so that he will discriminate between scents on articles when we want, will search for hidden articles as we wish, and will track at our request. Situations can be created which will give him the experience required to carry out all three requirements at will. Although a habit-forming approach is required to create the association in the dog's mind of the job in hand, experience under various conditions is of the greatest importance. He can only become reliable if we can guide this experience across a broad enough front and with sufficient depth to allow him to use the full scope of his inherited powers. Any sign on our part of using a domineering, overbearing or demanding approach will split his attention and affect the reliability we would hope to attain.

Nosework conditioning involves the requirements for three different end products:

1   Scent discrimination for obedience competitions builds up through three competitive stages.
2   Searching for working trials is graduated into two stages.
3   Tracking for working trials builds up through three stages.

If a handler decides to compete in both obedience and working trials, special precautions must be taken to ensure that the dog understands the difference between the scent discrimination and search exercises.

Part One – Scent Discrimination

This is an exercise where the dog is required to go out to articles which are visible to him, to identify and bring back the article bearing the scent he has been given. Although there can be a total of up to ten articles, only one will carry the particular scent he is after. Some of the other articles will carry the scents of other people – these are known as decoys. The procedure for each stage of competition is the same. The steward, without putting his own scent on the article, will take it out and place it amongst the other articles whilst the handler prevents his dog from watching the article being placed. The articles are usually placed about two feet apart and about five to ten paces from the handler.

The stages of competition become progressively more difficult, and all conditioning should be constructed to achieve the final requirement, Class C scent discrimination. The three competition stages are:

1 Class A. The handler's own article is used with the handler's scent on it and placed amongst a variety of articles.

2 Class B. The judge's article with the handler's scent, is placed amongst similar articles where the dog cannot visually recognise the correct one.

3 Class C. On this occasion clothes are used, about six inches square, and the dog is requested to discriminate and return the judge's scented article.

Although there are only three grades of competition, there are five major conditioning elements in progressing from the simple retrieve to Class C scent discrimination. Each of these elements is of importance, and failure to understand their requirements can well be the reason for the failure rate that is evident at any obedience show.

These conditioning elements are as follows:

a) Advanced retrieve – fetching a well-used retrieve article from a scattered group of miscellaneous objects. The purpose is to condition the dog to make straight for the scent discrimination area and to start the changeover from sight retrieving to scent seeking.

b) Scent discrimination for various dual-scented articles (those with the scent of the dog and handler) and then unused single-scented articles from the scattered group of miscellaneous objects. This will continue the change from sight retrieving to scent seeking and also from the handler and dog scent to handler scent only.

c) Scent discrimination of similar objects to eliminate sight retrieving and consolidate on handler scent.

d) Scent discrimination on cloths, introducing the administering of scent to the dog via scent cloth, by using the handler's scent.

e) Continuation of cloth scenting with the introduction of discrimination for a stranger's scent.

To save any confusion in the description of this conditioning programme, I shall use the word 'article' to indicate the scented one to be returned by the dog; the decoys and others will be called the 'objects'.

The approach for conditioning and creating the desired habits can only be based on a good keen retrieve, with Class A scent the first extension of the retrieve exercise. The initial purpose is to condition the dog to go out and look for the handler's own article amongst the scattered objects. The objects at all stages of conditioning should have other people's scents on them, but should never carry handler's scent. The more objects which are scented the better. If the dog becomes accustomed to decoy scents whilst sight seeking, and if this approach is maintained right through the conditioning process, the Class C decoys can become a non-event.

When a dog is released to go out and look for his thrown article amongst the decoy objects he will become accustomed to the uninteresting strange scents. When his regular article is then hidden behind an object his nose will start to take over and the other scented objects will just become part of the background scene.

The first conditioning element is that of the advanced retrieve of a thrown, well-used, dual-scented article lying amongst the scattered objects. Although some or all of these objects are well scented your dog will ignore them and visually seek out his own article. Two objectives are being satisfied –

118

that the dog knows his article will be somewhere amongst the objects, and that he shows a complete lack of interest in other scents, or the decoys. This process should not take long, in fact about three sessions should be sufficient.

The next stage is to leave the dog at the sit whilst you take the article out and place it behind an object to ensure that there is a higher probability of his nose picking up the scent before he sees his article. Remember that this is being carried out as an advanced retrieve rather than a scent discrimination exercise.

Now get a friend to take your article out, without handling it, and place it within the scattered group of objects. You can let the dog watch the procedure but before releasing him to go out to retrieve the article you cut off his vision, either by walking in front of him or turning him round before setting him up properly for the retrieve. Vary the position of your article amongst the objects and occasionally hide it behind one of them. When you are satisfied that he is using his nose when the article is not obvious you can start thinking about the approach to actual scent discrimination.

So long as your own articles are being used your dog does not need to be given your scent but to obtain the right conditioning, to let your dog know what is coming up, to prepare for the introduction of a Class C scent and to help differentiate between obedience scent discrimination and the working trials search, it is essential to go through some sort of procedure which will be of greater value at a later date. The normal and sensible approach is to cup your hands gently and loosely over the dog's nose and request him to 'Seek' and 'Fetch'. As he is accustomed to the fetch for retrieving he will consider this still to be some sort of retrieve. Gradually the emphasis can be put on to the instruction to 'Seek' and the cupping of your hands over his nose lets him know it is a scent discrimination exercise.

Until now your article has been dual-scented, by your dog's mouth and your hand, remembering that as soon as the dog has had the article in his mouth his scent is on it and thereafter it may be his own scent he is going for instead of yours. The introduction of fresh articles strongly scented by yourself, and either only used once or else newly washed, will bring home the full scenting requirement to discriminate for articles unknown to him.

A dog conditioned for the requirements already described will have no problems in dealing with a Class B discrimination where the scented article is identical to all the objects being used. Consolidation for this stage should not require many sessions, although you must remember to use as many decoy scents as possible. It is the best way of making decoys a non-event in this exercise.

Progressing on to a stranger's scent, as in Class C, requires a lot of consideration and should not be attempted until complete satisfaction is attained with a Class B scent. Until now the dog has been conditioned to seek out articles with your own or his own scent, and he has been encouraged to ignore a stranger's scent. In fact it has been a crime to consider returning with a stranger's scent. There are now two basic changes for the dog to contend with:

1   Although he has been given your scent from your hands so far, we do not know whether it means anything to him or not. Your scent is probably his best-memorised scent and the cupping of your hands over his nose will have had little to do with his scenting ability, but this procedure has prepared him for a stranger's cloth to be put over his nose so that he can now take note of the scent.

2   He has always gone out knowing that your scent will be out there on an article. He is now being expected to memorise a strange scent, discriminate and bring back the correct cloth.

If the dog is given both changes to contend with at the same time there is a fair chance he will become confused, and that is the last factor we would want to introduce. Progress is made therefore by introducing the cloths as objects and article. The

120

scent to be used is the one the dog knows so well, that of his handler. With decoys in the line-up as usual the dog should know the routine well enough and should not be unduly disturbed by the cloth being placed over his nose. It should not take long for a dog to become fully accustomed to this procedure or to the retrieving of a piece of cloth.

The introduction of another scent can now be made with the help of a friend to scent the cloths. Have your friend scent two cloths and give one to you. Handle it at the two top corners only and place it over the dog's nose. At the same time your friend draws attention to himself as he walks out about ten paces and lets the dog see him drop the other cloth. As soon as the cloth is dropped and your friend starts to step back out of the way, withdraw the first cloth from your dog's nose, release him, telling him to 'Seek', and as he reaches the cloth encourage him to bring it back to you. This is a straightforward retrieve. Repeat this procedure with fresh cloths and the same friend's scent. Two decoy cloths can now be placed on the ground whilst the process is repeated for a third time. Try to ensure that the dog is watching your friend place the cloth between the two decoys and then release him as before to 'retrieve' the correct cloth. During this period give your dog all the encouragement he needs. Always place the first cloth over his nose first to remind him of the scent he has to find.

At the next session use a different friend and repeat the process, but make use of the decoys after the first successful retrieve of the correct cloth and limit the number of friends to about three until the dog is fully confident of the process required. You should never use any of these three friends as decoys. When confidence has been built up, more decoys and 'dead' cloths can be added until the full total of ten can be placed in various patterns on the floor.

During this period your dog is being encouraged to watch the correct cloth being placed, but at the same time he will have had to discriminate to find the correct cloth. He should now be ready for the exercise in full, where he is prevented from watching the cloth being placed and he is given the scent first as the only identification.

The experience of various people's scents can now be extended to ensure that the dog can discriminate under all normal conditions. Care should be taken, however, to make sure that the friends used during the initial training period are not used also to supply decoy scents until the dog is well practised. Keep in mind that during competitions the judge and the decoy scents are generally those of strangers to the dog, and the discrimination should be relatively simple to a dog who has been properly conditioned.

Obedience competitors when training for working trials require to take special precautions not to confuse the dog between scent discrimination and searching.

Scent discrimination should be treated, from the start, as an advanced obedience retrieve exercise with full control, starting from the prescribed sit position, with conditioning sessions carried out on very short grass or smooth surfaces. With the search exercise, as explained later, a very free approach is applied and the dog should not be made to sit prior to the release for searching. When practising the search I advocate the use of short grass or smooth surfaces on occasions, but this should be avoided when scent discrimination is being considered.

It is very important that the conditioning processes are as far apart as possible.

Part Two – Searching

In this exercise the dog is required to cover an area of twenty-five yards square, marked off by four corner posts, and to find four articles placed by a stranger. The ground is usually of medium to long grass, light undergrowth or possibly heather. The time given is a maximum of five minutes and a minimum of two articles must be found. The regulations also state that the articles should be well handled and, for guidance, that they should be similar in size to a six-inch nail or a matchbox. The judge, however, does have the discretion of modifying the size of the articles to suit the nature of the ground. These details cover the search requirements for all the tracking stakes. The C. D. search only requires an area of fifteen yards square with three articles being placed in the area, but again two articles have to be found. The conditioning process to be explained is designed to cover the full searching experience required for the tracking stakes.

Good keen searching ability is, I think, the most useful attribute a dog can have. If we consider how often items get lost when out walking or playing with the children – the car keys, the house key, or perhaps a wallet or a piece of jewellery – a dog with the desire to use his nose is of far greater value than a dozen people using their eyes. When I played golf, my greatest expense was the replacement of lost golfballs: the fairways were always too narrow for my style of play. I then started taking my Quest out with me, and lost golfballs became a thing of the past, not because my style of play had changed but because I had a mobile golfball-detector with me. As this golfball-detector did not encourage me to change my golfing style and he was creating quite a reputation in the obedience ring and in working trials, I decided to concentrate on the more successful pastime.

Searching is, I think, the most misunderstood exercise in the complete working trials routine. Too many competitors treat it as a very serious exercise and train in a very serious manner. It is very apparent that the accepted obedience type of thinking goes into their approach for training. I recall one handler I helped from the start in trials work; he already had a good foundation on control work and his dog was keen to search. We guided this dog in a natural manner, and my friend was the envy of most handlers in having a dog who could work so keenly and so easily. We had built on an inherited attribute. This handler's second dog in working trials was trained in a different manner – he was going to be disciplined into working.

I have judged this dog on a number of occasions and know that the handler is ashamed of the searching performances his dog has given.

This does not mean that we do not take the exercise seriously and methodically. We are serious in ensuring that the dog is going to be guided in a manner which he will enjoy. He will not realise he is being asked to work, but he will be so conditioned that he will sense the occasion and find it hard to contain himself until he is released. As far as the dog is concerned it will be a game with a very pleased handler backing him up with any support required. Remember we are asking a dog to concentrate for a period of up to five minutes. He cannot and will not do it properly if his mind is affected by strict control or a nagging voice from outside the search area.

Instead of training a dog to search we mould his natural ability to suit our purpose. With some dogs the searching ability may not be apparent but the correct approach can draw this latent talent to the fore. Our training has gone into the retrieve, and if we have done the job properly we have a dog which is not only happy to retrieve but is always looking for the opportunity to go out and fetch articles as part of the fun in life. This is the real basis for a good sound search. We do not train a dog to search but condition him in such a manner that our approach tells him what is coming. He is then released to carry out a function for which he has both the ability and keenness.

What are we actually asking from a dog? We are asking him to work at distances up to twenty-five yards away from the handler and to cover the ground making full use of his scenting powers, so that he can pick up the scent from articles out of sight in the long grass or undergrowth. As each article has a human scent on it he should 'home' onto it, pick it up and return with the article to the handler. There are three main considerations in our conditioning programme:

1 To have the dog working quite independently of the handler and at a distance.

2   Complete concentration and dedication to the job in hand for a period of time which can be considered to be lengthy in comparison with any other exercise discussed up till now.

3   The recognition of articles scented by persons unknown to the dog and without previously being given the scent.

If a dog is initially trained to work close to the handler it becomes rather difficult to get him to work at a distance, and if he cannot be induced to concentrate for a short period he certainly will not be reliable for the time we consider necessary. The ability to pick up the scent of an article which has been handled by a human being should not cause any real problems, although there are times when insufficient scent on an article can make the job difficult – and who are we to know how much scent is on an article?

Before we go into the methods of conditioning, it should be noted that there is no formal start to the exercise, as with obedience exercises, neither is there a formal presentation of articles nor penalties as such for extra commands. There are marks for control and style, however, and marks can be lost for the handler keeping quiet just as easily as for talking too much and distracting the dog.

We can now look at the conditioning objectives required to progress from a simple retrieve to the full search exercise:

1   Scent retrieving on the handler's own article and also for a friend's article.

2   Searching for the handler's own articles or a friend's articles.

3   Searching in squares foiled by a person having walked in various directions over the area.

Scent retrieving is the expression I use to indicate an advanced retrieve where an article is thrown into an area of grass or undergrowth which ensures that the article has a reasonable chance of being out of sight. It is the use of the dog's sight which takes him into the general area but his scenting power which 'homes' him on to it.

By using the scent retrieving approach a sound foundation can be achieved on distance between dog and handler. A dog which only works round a handler's feet is useless, and the effort required to keep pushing a dog into the centre or to the far side of the square only makes a handler irritable and drains the working enthusiasm from the dog. The scent-retrieving can, therefore, be used to get a dog accustomed to working some fifteen to twenty-five yards from the handler. When this becomes a habit, he expects to be working some distance from the handler and he can be drawn closer without losing any of his enthusiasm.

We can now look at our conditioning objectives, keeping in mind that we wish to see the dog enjoy himself. Enough enthusiasm must be built up to ensure that he will search continuously for the required period and be working as well at the finish as he was at the start. This conditioning process should be treated as fun sessions where forceful control should not be necessary.

Conditioning starts with the dog on the lead. You excite him with a decent-sized article and then throw it well away from you. He will pinpoint the general area, and when released will use his sight to get there, then his nose will take over until he has found your article. If the article is thrown into the wind he should pick up the scent fairly quickly. Do not ask for a presentation when he brings the article back but take it from him and, whilst he is loose, throw it out for him to do a fun retrieve. (This free throwing also gives the dog an appetite for the game.) Then try throwing the article downwind to assess his ability to find the article. In this case he has to pass the article to get on to the windward side before he can pick up the scent.

Do not have him working too long in the wrong area, as it is essential that he does not give up. If he requires help, position yourself so that he can be drawn into the correct area; if it seems hopeless, move into the area yourself and drop an article without the dog seeing you, then finish on a successful note.

When you are satisfied with his progress hold your dog whilst you throw out two articles together. Although they will land reasonably close to each other he will mark one and even do a straight retrieve when released. On sending him back to seek out the second give him plenty of encouragement and if need be go out and help him. He has to get the idea that there is more than one article out there waiting to be found and to help get this idea right into his mind it is a good plan to throw three or four good-sized articles on to short grass or on to a smooth surface so that the articles are clearly seen by the dog, then release him to bring them back to you. This can be great fun, and it is remarkable how much of a hurry a dog can be in to go out again for the next article. This procedure being carried out in parallel with the scent retrieving will speed up the change-over to multiple article searching. However, dogs being prepared for scent discrimination should not be introduced to this part of the conditioning procedure and a slower pace should be accepted.

A friend's article can be introduced, but maintain the scent retrieving approach. When the dog understands that he should retrieve any article with a human scent additional articles can be thrown in by your friend, remembering to use only one person's scent within any one session. Also remember that once a dog has had an article in his mouth it becomes dual-scented. With a dual-scented article you do not know which scent is most prominent, which means that you do not know which scent is attracting him to the article.

Whilst he is working watch his every move and give him any encouragement he needs, especially when he seems to pick up the scent of an article. Let him know you are backing him up, but do not distract him with unnecessary chitchat. If you think he has not gone out far enough to wind the article do not try to push him out further but move round in a circle so that you can draw him into the area you wish to be covered.

Many trainers will say that you should train by commands

and by the use of single words for an exercise. Although obedience competitions make single-word commands a requirement, working trials nosework does not. I never send a dog out to search or track on a single word, be it command or instruction, but I do emphasise the main word or phrase as I release him to carry out the search exercise. I build him up with the question: 'Where is it?' and then release him with: 'You *find* it, son.' This approach also helps to prevent any harshness in the voice and takes away any suggestion of a command.

When your dog is eagerly scent retrieving four articles which have been thrown out one after the other whilst he has been watching, it is time to consider the next stage and to introduce the four marker posts for each corner of your twenty-five-yard square. Remember that the four corner posts are for your guidance only, and that these posts should mean nothing to the dog. He should accept them as part of the landscape and should not be troubled by the fact that they carry human scent. This objective is achieved by continuing with the scent retrieving process, but the stage is now being set for the placing of articles in the square rather than their being thrown in. This now adds the scent of the person having walked through the square and creates a slightly more complicated working atmosphere for the dog.

To build up and consolidate on working at a distance, use the far half of the square only. Take your three or four articles out, foil that half of the square and let your dog see you drop the articles well spread out in this half square, then return to him and immediately release him to go and find your articles. When you go out to place the articles in the square, tie the dog to a fence or let somebody hold him. Do not make him stay or inhibit him in any way, so that you can maintain the enthusiasm and anticipation you have been building up. Again use a friend on occasions to place articles with his scent on them and let your dog watch so that he knows it is not your scent he is going out for. Gradually increase the foiled area of the square and start dropping the articles so that the dog does not realise where they are. The dog is being conditioned to work where people have walked, and if he searches out of the square he is not doing anything wrong. If the wind is to your advantage make use of it, as he may well pick up the scent of an article near the edge of the square. On the other hand if the wind is of no benefit whilst he is out of the square position yourself to draw him in again.

Your dog should now be well conditioned to the square and the searching procedure and he can now be introduced to a search area without any prior knowledge of it. If your preparation for each search has been correct he will know exactly what is wanted of him, and experience of a wide range of friends and also of differing types of ground is now required to obtain the versatility needed for trials work.

Although there is no need at any stage to avoid the foiling of searching ground by other people the process should be purposely introduced when the dog has a reasonable amount of experience behind him. A friend with a dog should be encouraged, on occasions, to foil the searching area. A square should not, however, be used if another dog has recently fouled this area. There is a great difference between fouling and foiling.

During the whole of this conditioning period you should be training yourself to read your dog and to work him into the various areas of the square. Draw him to the left or right as required, and if you want him to work the area just in front of you, move back and draw him into the area, giving him room to work. If possible, keep away from the windward side of the square. Some trainers and judges say that you must never go round to the windward side of the square as your own scent will spread over the search area. They are perfectly correct, of course, but if it is necessary on the odd occasion to move to the windward side to ensure that the dog covers the ground, then I am afraid my sentiments are to get on with it. Finding the articles is more important than upsetting a judge who does not have a full understanding of this exercise.

I remember taking one young dog into his first C.D. search – only one article in a twelve-yard square. He saw the four marker posts for the previous competitor's search and I could see that he was determined to make that one his search square as well. I prepared him in the usual way, but on release he went immediately behind me to work the other square. I immediately ran round to the other side of my square, the windward side, recalled the dog and as he came into the area he winded the article, veered slightly to pick it up and returned straight back to me with it. All in twenty seconds from the start. The judge acknowledged the cause of the problem and awarded full marks for the manner in which the exercise was accomplished. The lessons from this encounter were simply that my scent being carried into the square had no effect on the dog's ability to pick out an article with my own scent on it. If I had not committed the cardinal sin of standing on the windward side, I doubt if I would have been able to push this dog into the correct square within the time limit.

Articles for searching can vary tremendously. Although the regulations are clear enough some judges tend to use ridiculously small articles, and it has been known for an inexperienced steward to drop the articles without giving them a reasonable chance of being scented. It is all too easy when competing to blame the judge or steward when a dog fails to return with the requisite number of articles. Think twice before openly blaming judge or steward, but also think twice before inwardly or outwardly blaming the dog. If his usual performance is normally good enough and he has worked hard for you on the day, what more can you ask of him?

Part Three – Tracking

I hesitate before I call tracking an exercise, even although it is obviously listed as one in the working trials schedule. Tracking is not something to teach a dog, but an art to be developed.

Watch any dog on the loose – an Alsatian, any other breed or even just a mongrel on the street – and he will track wherever he wishes. He will start tracking when something takes his interest and he will stop when he loses interest. If we therefore start with the premise that we cannot and do not need to teach a dog to track we have a good chance of controlling our approach so that we finish with a sound and reliable tracking dog. If we try to teach a dog to track, we shall probably be taking the easiest and quickest road to cancelling out any natural instinct he possesses.

We, as handlers, have much more to learn in the art of tracking than the dog, and if we consider all our tracking sessions as handler training and dog conditioning sessions we shall get off to a good start.

If a dog knows so much more about tracking, how do we bridge the gap between dog and handler? This can be achieved by recognition of three main objectives:

1   To condition the dog to track where and when we want and for as long as we want.

2   For the dog to gain the experience required to work out older and more complicated tracks, to remain on the selected track and to eliminate cross-tracks of any kind.

3   To learn, as handlers, to read and understand the dog's reactions, to assess ground and weather conditions and to acquire the ability to become the junior partner in the team. To guide the dog into a situation where he realises that the handler is completely dependent on and confident of the dog's tracking ability and self-control.

The Inherited Instinct

Like any other inherited instinct, a natural ability and desire to track varies considerably from one dog to another. Their power of concentration and the sensitivity of their noses are other major factors affecting the ease or patience required to condition dogs into tracking. In other words some dogs find tracking much easier and more interesting than others, and some with the best handlers available just do not have the ability to pick up faint scents with the ease of other dogs. However, I have yet to see an Alsatian who, with the correct build-up, was not a prospect to reach a reasonable competition standard, and it should therefore be considered that any Alsatian, as an unspoiled puppy, has the prospect of becoming a good tracking dog. It should also be recognised that as soon as a puppy leaves the nest we can affect his natural instincts by our own actions and attitudes.

A puppy or young dog should be allowed to use his nose if he wants to do so, not at lamp-posts or street corners but out in the open where there can be so many fascinating scents. This natural inclination should not be curbed unless he is moving beyond a controllable distance, but at the same time he should not be verbally encouraged until the proper conditioning process for tracking has been started. This natural inclination should just be allowed to happen.

I remember judging a T.D. Stake in which during the two days of tracking my wife was following me from one track to another accompanied by my young dog. This dog, who was often no more than five yards behind me, would insist on tracking me from field to field. He could see me perfectly well but had far greater pleasure tracking his adopted Dad all over the place. To let this dog think he was being a nuisance during that period would not have done me any good when it came to a more serious and purposeful approach to tracking.

What is Tracking?

This may appear to be a rather stupid question, but it is often asked. 'How do you lay a track?' is another. I think these are sensible questions, as tracking can be confused with the

132

activity of trailing, a sport very popular in certain parts of the country.

To keep it simple, a track is the scent left behind by a person who has walked over a piece of ground. It is the scent left or created by his footsteps on the ground, the human scent from his body or the scent from his clothes or boots being brushed against the undergrowth, along with the scent from disturbed soil or bruised vegetation. The objective is to have the dog pick up the scent of a person who has been in a particular area and follow the ground scent left by that person as he walked along. Also to identify any article dropped by that person along the scent track.

Tracking Requirements

The Working Trials Regulations can now be examined to find out just how we expect a dog to perform. There are three different competitive stages in tracking requirements, the one common factor being that of distance. Tracks at all stages of competition are approximately half a mile long and a post is put into the ground to indicate the start of the track. The main difference in grades of competition are:

Utility Dog (U.D.). A second post is put into the ground about twenty yards from the start to indicate the initial direction of the track to the handler. The track should be not less than half an hour old with one article at the end. The finding of this article is not a requirement for qualification, although the marks for finding it can be valuable. *Working Dog* (W.D.) and *Police Dog* (P.D.). The track should not be less than one and a half hours old and shall include two articles, one of which must be recovered to qualify. *Tracker Dog* (T.D.). The track should be not less than three hours old and shall include three articles, two of which must be recovered to qualify.

In W.D., P.D. and T.D., the articles should be evenly spaced along the track with the last article indicating the finish. It will be noted from these requirements that the track is the connecting link between the starting post and the various articles. By failing to find sufficient articles a dog cannot qualify and by failing to follow a sufficient length of the track a dog may not find the articles. The purpose of our approach to conditioning is to ensure that the dog is using the track to find the articles.

Competitive track shapes vary tremendously and normally include five to ten corners. These can be at any angle although most are either a right angle or more acute. Occasionally a corner may have a gentle curve rather than a positive sharp turn. The distance between corners (the legs of a track) can also vary considerably and they are normally between twenty and two hundred yards (or paces) apart.

Tracking Conditions

There are three basic factors which affect the scenting conditions:

1 Type of ground.
2 Weather conditions.
3 Time-lag between laying the track and working it.

These three basic factors plus others affect the strength of the various scents caused by a person walking on a piece of ground. We are now working in the realms of theory, and if we attempt to go too deeply it will probably become confusing and possibly misleading. Theories can have a habit of backfiring if there is not enough tangible evidence to support them.

For the purpose of appreciating what a dog is trying to sort out when tracking, we shall define some of the theories which seem to have a great deal of substance. When a person walks on a piece of ground the scents left behind can be considered from three different sources:

1 Body scent in the air which drifts and clings to the vegetation, probably extending some distance from the footsteps on the actual track.

134

2   Scent of boots and clothes brushing against the undergrowth or vegetation.

3   Bruised vegetation or disturbed soil.

On a very fresh track the scents from the three sources will be present and relatively strong. The longer the time between track-laying and the dog working, the more these scents become dispersed into the atmosphere. We do not know how many scents are created at each footstep nor do we know the varying strengths and prominence of each scent. It would appear that while the body scents, being rather dispersed, will probably diminish in strength fairly quickly, the scents from boots and clothes will probably weaken more slowly and will become a background scent compared with that of the bruised vegetation. Theory has it that bruised vegetation or disturbed soil maintains a scent for quite some time.

The length or density of any vegetation will have considerable effect on the strength of scents, and so will the condition of the vegetation. Nice sweet green grass will maintain a stronger and longer-lasting scent than grass in dry sun-baked conditions. Dampness in the ground holds the scent very well and a ploughed field will create better scenting conditions than hard, bare, dry earth.

I once laid a track on the beach at the high tide level (the tide had receded at the time). I walked along alternating a few times from damp sand to dry, then back to the damp sand. About half an hour later I put the dog on this track. The damp sand was very simple and he worked at a nice pace, but as soon as he moved on to the dry sand he had to work very hard. Each time the dog moved on to the damp sand the track was easy to follow but each time he reached the dry sand it was evidently a struggle to pick up any scent to follow. It was very apparent that dampness created the better scent-holding conditions and dry conditions considerably shortened the life of the scent.

It will therefore be recognised that weather conditions can have a tremendous effect on the strengths of track scents. With a drying wind on a sunny day the scents will disperse much quicker than on a damp still day. A thunderstorm can wash a track away within half an hour, whereas continuous rain may well create better scenting conditions.

Overall tracking conditions are basically determined by the ground, the weather and the time-lag between track-laying and working. A track left for ten hours overnight may be just as easy for a dog to follow as a three-hour track laid at mid-day. It will be appreciated that conditions change for every track and during every track. If we think too deeply into the subject we shall find many excellent excuses for failures but we shall find it very difficult to substantiate the reasons within climatic or ground conditions for these failures. Although it may be possible to assess such conditions reasonably well there are many unknowns. What wild game or people have crossed or run down the leg of a track just before or just after it was laid? Many good tracking dogs have unexplained failures in what appear to be good conditions. There are also times when conditions are expected to be extremely difficult and again the dog can prove the expectations wrong by making the track look easy.

Taking all these factors into consideration it would appear that a dog is quite capable of coping with and sorting out the scents which will enable him to retain the track's identity through quite a variation of differing situations.

Tracking Interference

Most tracks are affected by interference of some kind, because game, cattle, sheep or other humans may move across the ground either before or after the track was laid. Dogs that are permitted to chase rabbits and suchlike will have difficulty in concentrating on a human scent if the scent of these animals is around. Equally, tracks that have been laid over strong cattle scents can cause problems. On the other hand dogs with the correct guidance through the various stages seem to be quite immune to the various interference scents when they are present.

Although strong cattle or sheep scents can affect an inexperienced dog, the interference from a human being having crossed the track after it has been laid can create unwanted problems. I have returned to a track half an hour after laying it to find a family of four walking straight up the track towards the starting stake. If I had not witnessed this, how would I have reacted to my dog's inability to follow what should have been a simple track?

The secret is to know one's own dog well enough to trust him and reason that an unusual performance is probably because of interference of a nature which is too great for him to overcome. Until a dog has become an established tracker it is important that the handler knows precisely where a track has been laid, either by laying it himself or by having an experienced track-layer close at hand. Otherwise the handler has absolutely no means of knowing if the dog is following the correct track or changing over to some sort of interference.

Tracking Equipment

Although free tracking can be carried out and is good fun, free tracks play no part in present-day competitions. Tracking is therefore carried out with a harness fitted round the dog so that his shoulders can take any strain and his head has complete freedom of movement so that his nose can get right down to ground level. Some dogs are known as vacuum-cleaners because of the way they can settle down into a track.

The harness can be made of canvas or nylon webbing, although most people prefer a harness made of good-quality bridle leather. A good well-preserved leather harness will last a handler for his life time. If there is difficulty in obtaining a ready-made harness, the sketch in Figure 7 should help any good saddler to make one for you.

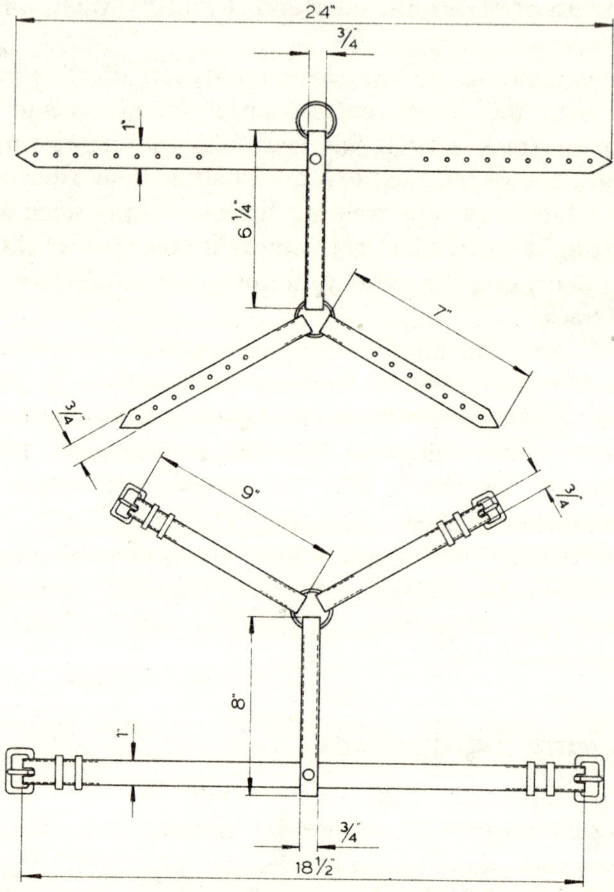

Fig. 7.   Tracking harness.

The tracking line is normally about twelve yards in length, with a clip at one end for attaching to the harness and a knot or loop at the other end for the handler to hold. Experience has shown that twelve yards is about the correct length: a shorter line can hamper a dog and a longer one add unnecessary weight and minimise the feeling of control. An ordinary washing line rope can be quite adequate but will rot in time; a nylon rope of similar diameter will last much longer. The P.V.C.-covered washing lines can be rather hard and are not really suitable.

The only other equipment required is two stakes. As four stakes are required for the search exercise, it is just as well to obtain six stakes so that the search can be worked whilst waiting for the track to be ready. Garden canes, broom handles or the like are quite satisfactory.

To Track – By Kind Permission of the Handler

As I have already stated at the start of this section, tracking is an art, not to be taught but to be developed. A properly prepared Alsatian requires no command, instruction or request to track. In fact any need for such an approach probably indicates that the easiest and best way of achieving a happy tracking relationship has not been obtained. It can be very misleading to watch a natural tracking dog go on to track with the command to 'Track'. The natural tracker would track without any command and may in the long run be inhibited by the use of such an approach.

The objective is to condition the dog to know when he is expected to track and then release him when ready. My own dogs know what is coming when they see me put the tracking harness into the car. They also anticipate tracking when I take a certain road through the hills, and it can become rather a nuisance with the noise they make in the back of the car. The dog always takes me to the tracking stake, and waits (often impatiently) until the harness has been fitted. The click of the tracking line being clipped on to the harness is the signal to track. It tells the dog he is being released and is permitted to seek out the scent in the region of the starting stake.

It may be a very short or rather long process to reach a situation where the dog knows exactly when he is expected to track, and it can be greatly dependent on the natural tracking instinct in the dog.

The Natural or Less-Motivated Tracking Dog

The tracking instinct in dogs can vary considerably, but within the Alsatian this variation is much narrower than one would expect if we were to consider all breeds. However, we still find within the breed that some dogs are natural trackers, and love to track anywhere and at any time. Then we have the dog who seems to have no interest at all in tracking; but with this dog we do not know the potential that is dormant and just waiting to be released. Just how do we tell if a dog is a natural tracker or not? This is quite easy, and with a very unsophisticated approach.

Take your dog on the lead, whilst out for a walk, and go to a field where there are absolutely no distractions. Tie him to a fence-post or something similar. Do not tell him to stay, just leave him and walk out about fifty paces or so then walk back down-wind in a semicircle (see Figure 8). Whilst he is tied up he may bark or jump around. Let him: do not scold him or inhibit him in any way. When you return to your dog untie him and repeat the walk with the dog on the lead. If he goes ahead of you with nose down, curious to know where you have been, he is a natural. He may only go twenty or thirty yards before losing interest or he may pull you right round until you return to the place he was tied up.

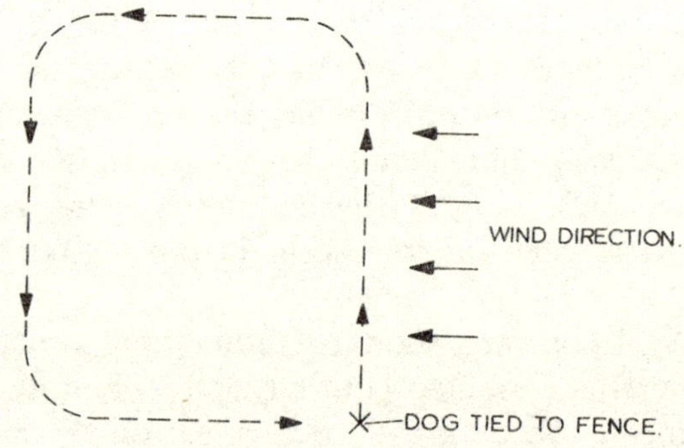

Fig. 8.   To determine the 'natural' or 'less-motivated' tracker.

If your dog is not seriously interested in investigating your track I would class him as a 'less-motivated tracker', and some sort of incentive will be required to create the desire to track.

Both types of dog can respond to a similar introduction to tracking, although the purpose of this introduction will be quite different. The 'natural tracker' needs no incentive to track, but in most cases he will not be interested in the article which may be left on the track by the track-layer. He can be built up into a highly experienced tracking dog without the finding of articles, but that is not the objective. The track must be used as a connecting link between articles and it is important for the dog to realise that he uses the track to find articles.

Many handlers make the mistake of working the 'natural tracker' to a high degree of effectiveness without troubling too much about articles. These dogs are generally very unreliable at indicating articles and, although beautiful trackers, can become a heartbreak in competition.

The 'less-motivated tracker' requires the incentive of something at the end of the track to induce him to make use of it to find that 'something'. The biggest problem with the 'less-motivated tracker' is that the handler will try to 'teach' him to track: many a potential tracker has been ruined by a teaching approach.

Inducement to Track

Tracking, or an article-finding inducement at the end of the track, can be applied by making use of a retrieve or a play article. It is a case of using the approach most suited to your dog. It is worse than useless to use the retrieve approach with a dog who is not happy in carrying out this exercise. The feeling of compulsion will ruin any chance of a happy and dependable tracker. The happy retriever will respond to his fun retrieve article at the end of the track so long as he has fun with it on completion of each track from the very start. The dog who does not retrieve can be found responsive to a play article, ideally some article used as a tug-of-war. The point is that the inducement to track for the article is the enjoyment on finding it and the fun immediately after.

With the 'natural tracker' we wish to ensure that he stops at the article and then realises that there can be greater joy in finding it than trying to track further at this stage. The 'less-motivated tracker' requires the play or retrieve article as an inducement to use his scenting powers and will initially be guided by sight until he realises that his nose can make a far better job of it. It will therefore be seen that there is a different purpose in mind when educating both types of dog. However, the same foundation can be used to condition the 'natural' and the 'less motivated tracker'.

Track-Laying

Should a handler lay tracks for his own dog or should he have friends lay the tracks? There are two schools of thought on this subject and results indicate that both can be right. A mixture of both approaches can also be satisfactory.

A handler laying his own tracks requires a great deal of self-control whilst his dog is working the track. It is easy for the handler to try and control the dog instead of encouraging him to develop his own tracking technique. It is too easy for the handler to indicate to the dog that he is coming to a corner or even to indicate the direction to take. The sensitivity of the tracking line can tell a dog many things. The tracking line must be treated as a one-way communication system – from dog to handler, never from handler to dog.

The handler can, however, learn a great deal by studying his dog, especially when the handler knows where the track goes. He should learn to read his dog. Does the dog overshoot corners with a following wind? Does he track parallel to the track when there is a cross-wind? With the precise knowledge of where the track has been laid, a handler can study reactions

142

because he is prepared for most of the situations as they arise. Most people believe that a dog who has been conditioned to track on the handler's own scent finds it difficult to change to a friend or stranger's scent. If the proper approach has been made, with each step carried out so that the dog knows what is expected from him, the change from handler tracks to that of a stranger will not create any problems. All the dogs I have worked were introduced and brought to a good tracking standard on my own tracks, but they have shown no change in attitude when presented with a stranger's scent. If I meet with any tracking problems during a dog's working career I immediately return to laying all the tracks for the dog until the problem has been sorted out. Tracking problems cannot be cured by having a friend or stranger lay the tracks unless that person is well experienced and is capable of giving the handler all the assistance he requires.

This now brings us to the school of thought that believes a handler should never lay a track for his own dog. Many good and experienced handlers believe this to be true. My own belief is that many good tracking prospects have been ruined by the use of track-layers who did not have the experience to give the handler the backing and knowledge required to teach him how to 'read' his dog.

An inexperienced handler with an inexperienced track-layer is a very poor combination. My advice to the beginner is to 'go it alone' if he cannot obtain the assistance of a good experienced track-layer, and good track-layers are usually handlers with sound experience from working their own dogs.

Tracking Foundation

Keeping the purpose of tracking inducement in mind, start the foundation work by building up enthusiasm and making use of letting the dog watch the laying of the initial tracks. The first tracks should be of a length to suit your dog – they may only be ten yards or they may be forty to fifty yards. There is no need to bother with a tracking harness or stake at this stage. A lead or slip chain (not as a choker) may be used, although it is worth considering the use of a collar to remove any association with the training of the 'control' exercises. Using the collar instead of a slip chain can also prevent any tearing of hair round the dog's neck. You can have a friend hold your dog or tether him to a fence (a benching chain is ideal for tethering). Let the dog know you have his fun article, get him excited and walk straight out into the wind (see Figure 9A) – this can be important in order to ensure that the natural tracker has no reason to track beyond the article. Your scent will not have travelled any further than the article. Walk back to your dog by exactly the same route as your track. This will give a mixture of a forward and a back track. In the very early stage this will not adversely affect your dog but must not be continued after the initial objective has been attained. The objective is to get him to use his nose and stop at the article.

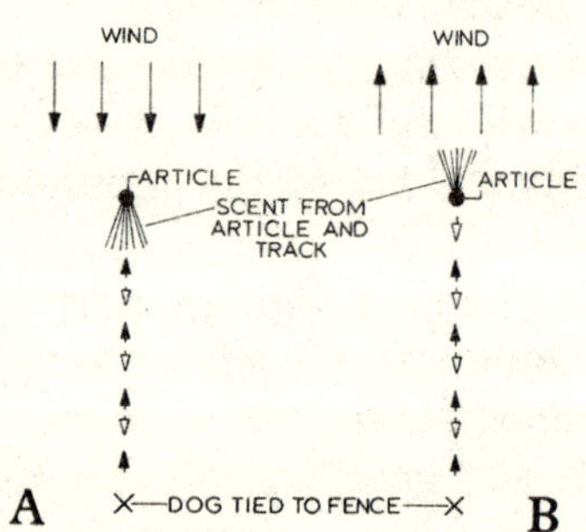

Fig. 9. Tracking foundation.

When your dog is prepared to recognise and stop at the article, which he does not require to pick up, similar short double tracks can be laid with a following wind as in Figure 9B. Although the track does not go beyond the article, the track and article scents will drift on some distance. Your dog should indicate the article as he passes it or within three or four feet of it. If he travels much further without an indication he is not fully prepared.

Although it is preferable to have your dog on a lead during this foundation stage, some dogs may respond better if the first two or three tracks are carried out free with a retrieve at the end.

Tracking Routine

When your dog is keen and happy to track out a short distance for his fun article it is time to consider the full tracking routine so that conditioning can be blended in from one stage to another.

We want the sight of the tracking harness, the line and the starting stake to cause your dog to become excited, so that he is anticipating the pleasure of tracking. Fitting the harness on the dog should create a certain amount of impatience, with the clipping of the line on the harness as the signal that he is being released to track. The harness should never be fitted on a dog until you are ready to track, and then only fitted within a few yards of the start of your track. Putting on the harness and clipping on the line replaces any command or verbal instruction to track.

Practical police work will often require a dog to quarter an area of ground to pick up the scent of the track, but as we are mainly concerned with competitive tracking where there is a stake in the ground to indicate the dog's starting point our procedure will be based on the competitive requirements.

On tracking to an article your dog must indicate the presence of it very clearly – he may lie down beside it, stand over it or pick it up and bring it back to you. On finding the last article on a track the harness is immediately removed to let the dog know he is not required to track any further. It should be noted that a dog wears the harness only when he is tracking, never whilst he is waiting for a track or after it is finished, be it failure or success.

This tracking routine is the procedure we wish to apply when your dog knows what is expected of him. We do, however, bend a number of rules during the early training sessions to blend with the correct associations.

Learning the Routine: Assuming that a good foundation has been laid, and your dog understands that a line of scent leads him to an article he is keen to find, the next series of tracking sessions are aimed at cultivating the desire to track as soon as the harness has been put on. It would be wrong at this early stage to inhibit the enthusiasm we are trying to build up by fitting the harness *after* the track has been laid. The handler should have the tracking line laid out in readiness and the harness fitted on the dog immediately before laying the track. Once the harness is on, the dog should be tethered by means of a benching chain and collar to a fence-post or held with a lead by a friend. You then go out into the field a little way from him, put a starting stake in the ground and lay a short straight track (see Figure 10). The sight of the stake being put into the ground and of the track being laid gives the dog an added stimulus to track. As soon as you have laid the track, return immediately to the dog, remove his collar, clip on the line and encourage him as he puts his nose down to track. The tone of voice is more important than the words that are used. I usually say something like: 'That's a good boy, where is it?'

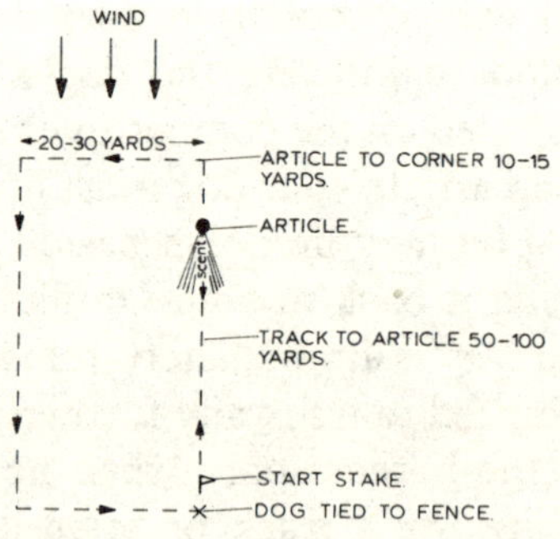

Fig. 10.   Learning the routine.

One or possibly two short tracks with the same routine will be sufficient during a single session, and one session in a day is enough. At first all tracks should be laid into the wind, so that your dog will be encouraged by winding the scent of the article before he reaches it. Progress of course depends on his enthusiasm and his ability to indicate the article's presence in a very positive manner. Similar tracks can then be laid with a following wind and then with a cross-wind. Before each track your dog should be tied to a fence-post or held by a friend, but with the freedom to get excited about the track being laid.

A corner can now be included and the track lengthened to somewhere between 100 and 150 yards. Once again lay the first leg into the wind so that the corner will be indicated by a dead end. There will be no scent beyond the corner and your dog will start to cast round to find the direction of the next leg. Although the article should not be left too close to the corner, it should be near enough to give your dog the pleasure of knowing that he was correct in taking the turn (see Figure 11). Again, progress should result in laying similar tracks with following and then with cross-winds.

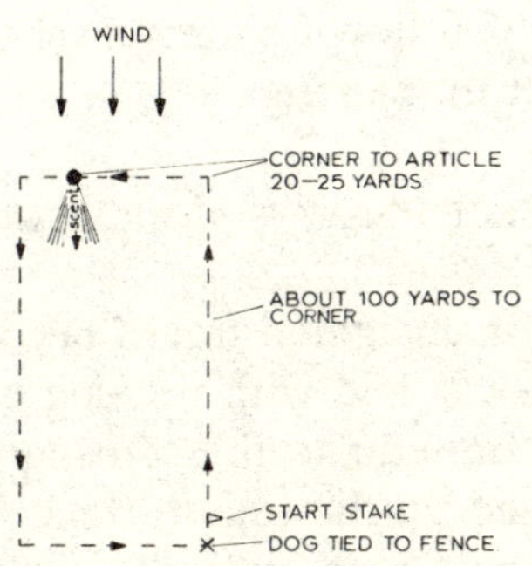

Fig. 11. Taking the first corner.

During all this build-up period the harness has been fitted on the dog immediately prior to the track being laid and removed after some fun on finding the article. By the time your dog has shown that he can concentrate long enough to finish strongly on the tracks already described he is ready to accept the fitting of the harness after the track has been laid and immediately prior to its being worked. The fun and games period immediately after finding the article can also be curtailed and the harness removed. Then have more fun with his article.

The dog should still be in sight of the track being laid. It is still worked fresh but has by now been extended to 200 to 300 yards with possibly two corners. By this time the fitting of the harness and the clicking of the line clip will have become the signal and release to track. A time delay can now be introduced and, although the dog may still watch the track being laid, a few minutes should be allowed to elapse before fitting on the harness. Assess the time delay to ensure that none of the enthusiasm for tracking has been lost.

The maintenance of tracking enthusiasm is more important than achieving long tracks or time delays. This observation is most important during the complete working life of the Alsatian. If enthusiasm diminishes during the last fifty yards or so then the track is too long, too old or both, and the next should be much easier, with particular attention paid to subsequent tracks. The following formula should be considered as an important factor in tracking:

TRACK LENGTH $+$ TIME DELAY $=$ CONCENTRATION REQUIRED.

The introduction of unsighted tracks becomes an important cornerstone. The track is laid with the dog out of sight and he is then immediately brought to the starting stake, the harness fitted and then released on the line to track. If the earlier part of the programme has been carried out there will be an immediate and excited response from the dog. The routine has been developed and the dog knows exactly what is wanted when the tracking harness is fitted.

Tracking Articles

As the incentive to track is to find articles, it is important to build up initially with a very limited number of good-sized articles which are well known to the dog. These articles should represent fun at the end of the track, and one of them should be very special. This is the article the dog knows best and can later be used as a 'saver'.

The saver is the article which is placed about ten yards beyond the last article on most non-competitive tracks to ensure that the dog finishes on a successful note. Where it is not used as a saver the article is carried by the handler to be given to the dog to play with on completion of the track. During the early tracking sessions the saver is the last article on the track and is only relegated to the position of saver when the dog has progressed far enough to recognise smaller and strange articles on the track.

The articles used on tracking can vary tremendously. Some judges use ridiculously small articles and at times track-layers tend to forget that the article should carry his scent. To take an article out of a plastic bag and drop it is not really good enough. When I am laying a track with more than one article to be dropped, I carry one in my hand and the remainder loose in my pocket. As soon as I have dropped one article, I take the next one and hold it until it is time to drop the second one, and then repeat the process as required. The articles can be of fabric, metal, wood, rubber, paper, plastics – almost any substance but certainly not food. The use of a matchbox, bottle cork or motorcar sparkplug should give some indication of a reasonably sized article.

When changing over from the favourite articles that are well known to the dog, drop each new article on the leg of the track whilst walking into the wind. This will give the dog a good chance to pick up the scent of the article before he reaches it.

Fuller Tracking Experience

When a dog has sufficient experience to tackle a half-mile track at half an hour cold without any problems and with great enthusiasm, both dog and handler are ready for blind tracks. These are tracks being laid by a third party without the handler watching where it has been laid or receiving the direct assistance of the experienced track-layer.

This is now where the evidence of handler self-control comes to the fore. Will he allow his dog to work out the track without trying to influence him in any way? Will the handler acknowledge that his dog knows best? If the handler did not see the track being laid how can he possibly know where the track went? As soon as a handler doubts his dog's ability the dog will start doubting and confidence will drain from both members of the partnership.

I can well recall one handler I helped in his early days. At his first trials in the U.D. Stake his lack of trust and faith in his dog's ability caused him to pull his dog off the track – he would not let the dog go in the correct direction. This handler thought he knew better than his dog. After this fiasco, I laid one track each week for this dog. They were not difficult tracks for the dog, but I went places the handler just did not expect. I would crawl under bushes, go through a fence, along the side of a fence and back again, along the side of a disused railway line, across and back along the other side. Every time the handler doubted his dog I was right behind to ask him why. After a few weeks this handler was prepared to follow his dog anywhere. He has now trained two working trials champions.

Another friend who comes out regularly with me knows that the track is likely to have some unusual feature, not to test the dog but to keep her alert and be prepared for anything at trials. One example was the use of a fir-cone as an article. Whilst laying the track I realised that I was walking under a fir-tree with cones scattered over the ground. I dropped my own cone under the tree amongst the other cones, and although this would not cause the dog any problem the situation had the handler thinking as her dog stopped and stood over the article – she could see nothing but scattered fir-cones. A less experienced handler would have told the dog to get on with the track, but this handler encouraged her dog to indicate the correct article. It so happened that my cone was from a different type of fir-tree, and she returned with the correct one.

Success breeds confidence. It is therefore important to plan each track to ensure that the risk of failure is minimal. Time and distance should be gradually built up with more corners – four to seven should be considered sufficient for most non-competitive tracks. Start some tracks with a short leg, say thirty

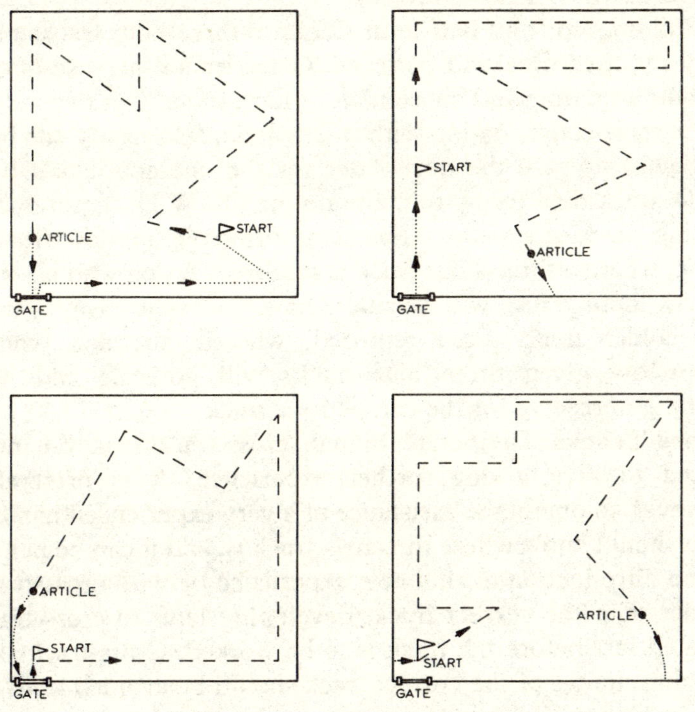

Fig. 12.   A variation of tracks.

yards, and start others with a very long leg, say 300 yards. Vary the directions and angles of the corners, especially the first corner.

If you, like most of us, have limited ground, do not make a habit of starting to lay the track from the same spot each time. If you use a field, start on different days from different sides of the field. If, after laying a track, your track-layer can get out of the field by a different route from entry, do so. If you can take your dog into the field by a clean route (where the track-layer has not been) then do so. Figure 12 will give you four examples when using the same field. Given sufficient thought it will be seen that the variations of approach within a single tracking area are almost inexhaustible.

Building up from half-hour tracks to three-hour tracks or so only requires time and patience. Consider an increase of half an hour at a time and consolidate. I have found that beyond the U.D. stage consolidating with tracks at approximately one hour cold will prepare the dog better for the one and a half hour W.D. track than trying to maintain the full W.D. requirements during practice sessions. The same principle applies with the T.D., where a three-hour track is required. A dog who is sound on two-hour tracks will normally have the enthusiasm to work the colder track when required, whereas the dog who is repeatedly given three-hour tracks will go stale and have nothing in reserve for the competitive track.

Cross-Tracks: Deliberate human cross-tracks can be introduced to give a dog further experience. It is preferable, however, to obtain the assistance of a very experienced handler. You should know where the cross-track is, and it can be helpful if the introduction to this new experience be with cross-tracks colder than the correct track, developing later to cross-tracks created just before the track is to be worked. Cross-tracks laid within minutes of the correct track should be avoided until the dog is well experienced and reasonably capable of countering such a difficulty.

The dog will probably indicate the area of interference and

may even check it out. If he investigates much more than the length of the tracking line without correcting himself, call him back. Do not pull on the line, take him back to the point of interference and cast him slightly beyond the cross in the correct direction. The fact that he took the cross-track must be taken as failure, so do not confuse your dog by asking him to try and work it out again. The area will probably be contaminated with your own scent. After a failure another deliberate cross-track should not be given until a few normal tracks have been given and successfully worked.

Chapter Eight

Working Trials

Organising

The successful running of trials depends to a great extent on the preparations made prior to the event, many of these arrangements requiring to be dealt with well in advance. Most established societies normally have set weekends in the year for their open and championship events and this pattern is so well established that the regular competitors know where and when to expect their choice of venue and can plan accordingly.

Application to hold championship trials is made to the Kennel Club by the end of June during the year preceding the trials. This allows the Kennel Club to allocate dates, and secretaries can then confirm arrangements they have already made. Open trials can, however, be applied for and arranged at much shorter notice. Judges are normally booked about a year in advance to ensure that the persons in question are available and that adequate time is given for Kennel Club approval.

A society breaking new ground, or dates, may well have to make a few 'contacts' to ensure that venues are obtainable. The availability of tracking ground can raise many problems, as it will require an area equivalent to the size of two eighteen-hole golf courses to accommodate the tracking entry for most trials. The 'contacts' for authorisation to use this sort of area may well be the owner, the tenant, the shepherd, the farmer or the parties holding the shooting rights. The control work venue is generally much simpler to arrange and may only require an application to the local authority or a sports club for suitable facilities.

Track-layers and stewards require to be contacted for availability. It is important to ensure that these helpers are not competing in the stake in which they are being asked to assist.

The schedule for championship trials needs to be prepared in time for Kennel Club approval well in advance of distribution. A list of prospective competitors is compiled from the members' list, from previous catalogues and any others likely to be interested. The schedule and entry forms are usually distributed about six weeks prior to the event, with the closing date for accepting entries at least three weeks before the trials. This gives time for the customary ballot for tracking times, notification of these times to the competitors, and also the printing of the catalogues.

As judges usually travel some distance, accommodation must be arranged, and most societies find it convenient to have judges booked in at a hotel which can be used as a base for the trials. In this way judges, officials and competitors can enjoy socialising in the evenings after a good day's work.

Running on the Day

Working trials are seldom a one-day event. Open trials generally take in two or three days, although competitors usually have the opportunity of completing all their work in one day. Championship trials are normally run over three or four days, with all dogs attending on the last day for the control work and C.D. Stake, and each dog in attendance on one of the previous days to carry out the track and search exercises.

At open trials dogs complete all their work in one day, and this can create a considerable strain on the organisation, with timing and competitor cooperation of vital importance. There may be a few miles between the tracking venue and the control work, and as a continuity of competitors is required at both venues it is of prime importance to ensure that the afternoon tracking competitors have completed their control work earlier in the day and vice versa. Some competitors are prone to do their control work when they please and cause congestion or delays at the end of the day. It is up to the organisers to ensure that competitors know when they are expected to report at the different venues, thus avoiding unnecessary delays. It is then the responsibility of the competitor to make sure he is available as and when required. A few societies do, however, run their championship events in the same manner as that described for open trials.

Championship trials can normally be run at a more leisurely pace, although timing is still of the utmost importance to ensure that each competitor is called up and has the opportunity to track at the correct time. Track-layers must also be time-conscious, to ensure that tracks are laid to the programme, which can, of course, be upset if the stewards are not available to guide competitors to the correct tracking area at the correct time.

As most championship trials reserve the last day for control work, and criminal work if a P.D. Stake is scheduled, the full organisation is then concentrated in one area. This last day is normally a Saturday. Although C.D. is the junior stake, it receives limited attention from some societies. The judge appointed is often one who is at the threshold of a judging career and may not have a full appreciation of his programme and the effect of delays. Under these circumstances a very sound organisation with a good steward is essential to give the support required. This is especially so when a P.D. Stake is scheduled, as it is necessary to complete the C.D. work by early afternoon so that the criminal work can commence. It is not fair to ask some of the C.D. dogs to work during the excitement of the criminal work.

The secretary usually finds that the tracking days need little attention, providing the society has a good trials manager. On the final day the secretary rarely has a minute to spare. A continuous stream of marking sheets flows in, and it takes time and patience to transfer these marks to the master boards. A flustered secretary, especially when intercepted by competitors wanting to know their marks, can produce wrong additions, mistaken qualifiers and placings.

A thoughtful judge will try to arrange the control programme so that the marks for individual competitors can be handed to the secretary as they are finished. In this way certificates for qualifiers can be made out as marks are totalled up, and it can minimise the time that competitors have to wait around at the end of the day for the presentation of prizes and qualifying certificates.

Judging

The judge is the person in the centre of all this activity, the person to whom the competitors look to expect a fair chance to qualify, and the person the organisers hope will work to their timetable and all the other arrangements.

The judge's responsibility starts with his planning of each exercise. Conditions on the day may change – that is outside his control. What he can plan is to give each dog as equal a chance as possible. The stiffness of the exercises and his marking should be such that each performance will receive its just reward. It is quite easy to plan within the regulations and yet create situations where it would be unreasonably difficult for a dog to qualify.

The planning of tracks and searches, and the articles to be used on these, can depend a great deal on the type of ground available. A judge may be given a description of the ground prior to the trials and can select his articles accordingly, but there can be occasions when the type of ground is not quite as anticipated. A wise judge will take spare articles in case he finds that his selection is not really suited to the conditions.

On the day of the trials, or the evening before, the judge will get together with his chief track-layer or steward and present the details of his tracks and articles etc. Although he has the full authority and responsibility for his arrangements he will be wise to listen to any comments on local conditions and then carefully consider the suitability of his plans. The track-layers and stewards will, of course, work to the judge's instructions.

The organising society arranges the sequence of nosework exercises and decides whether the track follows the search or vice versa, or if the searches are to be carried out in groups. Although there does not seem to be any rule giving societies this privilege, a judge is expected to fall into line. Different societies find that their own approach suits them well and can then perfect their organisation through the experience of each event. A judge is therefore wise to accept this recognised privilege: he already has plenty of scope in arranging the control and agility exercises in the order he wishes. He should also give consideration to the secretary by arranging his routine so that he does not present him or her with all the marks on completion of the stake – after all there is more than one stake and he is not the only judge.

A judge is only considered as good as his last appointment, and a good reputation built up over a period can easily be destroyed by a thoughtless, inconsiderate or inconsistent performance. Past experience has shown that, on average, three quarters of the competitors fail to qualify and will go home with some measure of disappointment. A pleasant and constructive attitude from the judge can make a competitor feel that his entry was worth while and not a waste of time and money.

Lastly, the judge's responsibility has not finished until he has written his report for the *Dog Training Weekly*.

Competing

The system of open and championship trials has been built up over a number of years whereby dogs are required to qualify through each open and then championship stage of U.D., W.D. and T.D. Stake. There is no need to qualify through P.D. Open to be eligible for P.D. Championship.

C.D. is the beginner stake, and although it is not compulsory it has been found to be a very useful introduction for obedience competitors who are thinking of breaking into the trials field of events.

The trials enthusiast has the advantage over the obedience competitor in that winning a stake is not a necessity for progressing up the competitive ladder. So long as the dog qualifies through open and championship trials with the certificate of merit or qualifying certificate he is eligible for the next stage. Although everybody likes to win, the only time the first prize ticket is of any real value is on winning the P.D. or T.D. Championship Stakes, where two tickets under different judges will result in the dog becoming a working trials champion.

Although the working trials system encourages a progressive training programme, a fair number of competitors feel that upon qualifying in one stake they must enter the next available trials in the higher stake in an attempt to gain further awards. This is often done without any thought of the dog's capabilities or of the need to consolidate before progressing to the higher stake. Each trials competitor should make an honest assessment of his dog's working standard before attempting the higher level of competition.

It is hoped that the previous sections in this chapter have helped the competitor to appreciate the amount of time and effort put in by a number of dedicated people to make working trials a success. It is all done for the benefit of the competitor. It may be found that some organisations do not match up to their responsibilities or that some judges can be rather discourteous and upset the beginner trying to do his best. However, the competitor also has his responsibilities. If he enters a particular society's trials under a particular judge he should fully honour his part of the agreement with the spirit we have come to expect from most trials enthusiasts.

Competitors, quite rightly, are out to enjoy themselves, but some fail to appreciate the problems created or the injustices felt by the organisers and judges due to the lack of knowledge of the regulations. There are also times when common courtesy is forgotten by the competitor during the period of disappointment after the failure of an exercise.

There are times, however, when one wonders if the trials organisers have read and understood the regulations, just as there are also occasions when a judge's knowledge of the regulations is in doubt. Two wrongs do not make a right, and the competitor adding ignorance to error does not help to ease any tricky situations which may develop. A competitor at one trials can be an organiser at another or even a judge, and he will understand the need for the fullest cooperation between all concerned to make the trials a successful event.

There are a few points worth considering to help the competitor realise his full responsibility.

The competitor's first responsibility is to his dog and devoting his attention to his dog's needs. Is the dog ready for the stake? Is it worth the cost and time to travel some distance to compete? Remember that every failure contributes to the next failure and a run of failures cannot be blamed on the judges, track-layers, stewards or anybody else. A string of failures may well be due to the lack of understanding as to why the first one occurred, and sound reasoning about the first failure could have prevented repeats.

The competitor's next responsibility is to the judge. Remember he entered accepting this person because his judgement was respected. For some sound or unexplained reason the dog may fail to qualify, and under these circumstances it is hoped that the competitor's respect for the judge has not altered. It can also be rather discourteous to the judge, unless permission was requested for a leave of absence, for a competitor to go away home after failing in the nosework

160

group, with no intention of returning to complete the control and agility exercises. Remember that the judge is there for the competitor's benefit and is probably giving up three days of his time to officiate at these particular trials. Quite apart from any discourtesy, it is against the regulations to withdraw without giving notice to the trials manager.

A late competitor will do more than upset the organisation, he may well incur disqualification, especially if late for the track and most certainly if late for a group of stay exercises. Failure to turn up for a track is one of the biggest crimes in my book. A breakdown en route cannot be helped, but a number of competitors know in advance that they cannot manage but make no attempt to contact the secretary or trials manager. I do not think it is fully appreciated just how much work goes into track-laying, and I am sure that the culprits would be rather annoyed if they arrived at some other trials and were told: 'Oh, we forgot to lay a track for you.'

A number of competitors expect the track-layer or search steward to go looking for articles their dog has failed to find. The organisers seldom have the time for this sort of activity, and are not obliged to do so. I have seen search stewards help a competitor to look for such 'missing' articles and fail to find them only to hear the competitor say: 'Even the steward could not find the articles,' with the obvious implication that the articles were not placed in the search area. These insinuations are usually based on the competitor's inability to accept his own or his dog's shortcomings. These few competitors should learn to accept their failures gracefully. Ours is a sport enjoyed by many, but it can be spoiled by a few.

Chapter Nine

Obedience Shows

Organising

Although the organising and running of an obedience show differs from working trials, the forward planning of the event is just as essential, and some of the arrangements have to be made a full year in advance of the show.

The show calendar is a very full one and a late application to the Kennel Club for the chosen date may well result in disappointment. As some of the judges chosen by the committee may be in demand elsewhere, an early invitation is again advisable – many judges are booked at least a year in advance. In this day and age each class generally requires a separate judge, and with the size of entries for some classes it is now essential to appoint enough reserve judges to accommodate the splitting of these large classes. The reserve judges may, however, compete at the show if they are not called upon to officiate.

Venues have become increasingly difficult to obtain and to keep for future events. Indoor and outdoor venues are being lost, some with justification, because of the general anti-dog feeling that has become apparent. It only requires the undesirable actions of a minority of thoughtless competitors to ensure that a venue is no longer available.

162

The full distribution of schedules is no longer the function of our postal service. The escalation of costs has altered this well-established procedure and a fair amount of ingenuity, with hard work from show secretaries, has resulted in the distribution of many schedules to the regulars at shows just prior to the event. The closing date for entries seems to hold some sort of fascination for competitors in all forms of 'dog' activities. The majority of entries seem to be received at the last possible moment. This invariably gives the show secretary quite a headache. There will probably be about two weeks left to the day of the show after the entries close, with the printing of catalogues to be arranged and the judges to be notified of the entries in their respective classes.

Rounding up helpers for the day can be quite a problem when everybody in the club seems to be wanting to enter his local show. Somehow the usual stewards find that, once again, they are in the thick of it. They either leave their dogs at home or take a little time from their duties to give the dog a quick competitive run-through. This lack of attention to their own dogs will certainly minimise the chance of these 'helpers' finishing high up in the tickets, and all because of their conscientious approach to the running of the show.

As the presentation of 'specials' is now a standard practice, secretaries have the added chore of writing to the various pet food manufacturers etc. for donations. When it is considered that special prizes are normally awarded to fifth place and that it is likely to be a ten-class show, we can see that some fifty special prizes require to be sorted out.

Running on the Day

As far as the organisers are concerned the show starts some three hours or so before the advertised starting time, especially with an indoor venue where access to the hall is not obtained for the evening before the show. The rings have to be arranged and score boards etc. have to be put into place. Shoddy preparations will result in a poorly-run show where little seems to go right. Everybody will feel the effect of this inadequacy, where one complaint will encourage another. However, a well-prepared show will run smoothly, there will be no serious complaints and nothing to encourage the string of minor grumbles that can make a secretary wonder if it is all worth while. This is the type of show where the majority take it all for granted without any realisation of the effort and planning involved.

The catering ladies carry a thankless burden, slaving behind the counter or by the cooker and never getting the opportunity to see what is going on at the ringside. Secretaries survive, but only just, under the continual pressure after the long build-up of all the prior arrangements. If they are found to be a little short of temper then make allowances and gracefully withdraw from their 'scene'.

The show manager, if he is properly organised with his stewards working efficiently, will appear to have the easiest job on the day. If he does, he has worked for it and deserves the confident composure, but no doubt he will be watching and anticipating problems before they arise.

The judges will welcome refreshments at the appropriate times. Although shows cannot run without competitors, satisfied judges will help to create satisfied competitors and therefore a happy show.

Judging

An obedience judge does not require quite as much forward planning as the trials judge but he is certainly under a more sustained pressure during his judging stint. A good steward will ease the burden, but judging forty to sixty dogs in one day requires continued concentration over a lengthy period. A judge will make mistakes or misjudgements, he will also be accused by 'knowledgable' ringsiders of various failings, but so long as he has the courage of his convictions and is genuinely fair he will not be condemned for being human. It is said that the only person who never makes a mistake is the person who never makes a decision.

A judge's first consideration is to arrive at the show in plenty of time to ensure that he has everything ready for the advertised starting time. There is much controversy about competitors not turning up at the starting hour, and although much of this criticism is valid I am sure the rot set in because of late judges. Judges must bear in mind that a late start will probably mean a late finish. It is extremely difficult to try and make up time as the day goes on and it is also unfair to the competitors. The controversy relating to competitors not attending at the starting hour is an age-old problem that seems to have got worse over the last few years. It could be resolved by a more determined approach from judges with the backing of the organising committees. I do not think it requires much ingenuity, only determination, to call the wayward competitor's bluff, and this problem of missing competitors during the first hour or so could be solved.

Many judges bring their own stewards with them, and this is where good teamwork can be very evident, with both organisers and the competitors reaping the benefit. A courteous judge and steward can help to make an obedience competition a real pleasure.

Show reports from judges are most welcome and I feel it is the duty of every judge to submit a report to the 'dog press', the *Dog Training Weekly* being the most widely read magazine for obedience enthusiasts.

Competing

Much time and effort goes into the preparing and running of an obedience show, and it is all for the benefit of the competitor. The broad details have already been written into the chapter on working trials and I would only be repeating myself to write it again. However, there are major differences between competing in obedience compared with trials, and these differences affect the competitor's mental approach.

The obedience competitive system is, in my opinion, not as conducive to a sensible training approach as that for working trials, and therefore the obedience competitor is not as fortunate as his counterpart in trials. As I see it, there are two very decisive factors which favour the trials competitor.

First, the most junior tracking stake brings in almost every exercise required for the most advanced work in the T.D. Stake, the only additions being directional control as an extension to the send away, and also Speak on Command. The P.D. Stake does, however, bring in a completely new field with the addition of criminal work. This is a specialised area and relatively few civilian competitors venture into it. The building up from U.D. through W.D. to T.D. only requires consolidation and a wider experience of the same exercises. The obedience competitor, however, is continually required to learn new exercises as he progresses from Novice through Classes A and B to Championship Class C.

Second, the obedience competitor has to win his way through every class until he is eligible for Championship Class C. The trials competitor is not dependent on the performance of others to determine his progress through the various levels. He need only concentrate on his own performance and a qualifying mark guarantees the opening to progress through to the next stage. Although this form of qualification may sound easy it must be appreciated that seventy to eighty per cent of the competitors, on average, fail to obtain a qualifying mark.

It will therefore be seen that the trials competitor will get his just reward for each good performance, while his obedience friend can toil from show to show, with excellent performances, but find that one other competitor at each show with a better performance is enough to maintain the stagnation at his current grade of competition.

Both these factors control the approach to training and the

attitude, within obedience circles, towards the need to win, especially in the lower classes. This drive to win in the Beginners and Novice classes where the entries are mainly between thirty and sixty dogs (a class must be split if the entry is greater than sixty dogs) is very great indeed. It is not uncommon for a dog to receive full marks only to find that there are two, three or more in the same position. Some dogs are known to have been unplaced after a full-mark round because of failing in the run-off for first place.

This situation drives a great number of competitors into the trap of concentrating on a limited number of exercises in an attempt to achieve absolute perfection and a robot type of performance; the dog then becomes bored and the handler frustrated. The competitors who are sensibly advised or can think more constructively will take a broader view on training and will include the foundation work for all obedience exercises during their Beginner-Novice stage. They may even find that their progress out of Novice has been enhanced because of the variety of work that has prevented boredom and frustration from taking control of the situation.

The answer to this problem is in the hands of the competitors and their club trainers but could be helped enormously if a solution could be found to control competitors' progress without this need to win so many of the lower classes. Under the old regulations where there was greater freedom in the choice of classes, I never won a Beginner class and only once won a Novice class, and only with one dog. This did not prevent me from taking my fair share of prize tickets in the higher classes, and my obedience training throughout was based on the gradual build-up for each exercise in the higher classes.

We now come to the day of the show, and the problems a competitor can cause if he does not give full consideration to the judge or the show organisation.

The first hour of a show is the most crucial period: time lost at this stage normally means a late finish to the show. A minority of competitors who seem to dislike early entry into the competition ring have now created a situation where the majority of competitors do not wish to work during the first hour or so of the show. I am sure they must be the same competitors who complain bitterly about shows running late. If a show does not start on time with a constant flow of competitors then it must finish later than planned.

This obvious reluctance on the part of many competitors to work early has caused so much concern that the Kennel Club Regulations have been modified to try and combat the situation. They now state that competitors should book in at the ringside within one hour of the starting time. Since the introduction of this change I have judged a Beginner class where one could expect the newest of competitors to be keen to get into the ring for their workout. The competitors were quite happy to book in, but were not interested in working. It was a wet, miserable October day and an out-of-doors show, but the competitors did not seem to be the least bit concerned that the judge, unpaid, and after a 130-mile journey, was going to be standing in the rain all day for their benefit. Although I was not conscious of it, I sometimes wonder if my marking on that day reflected my annoyance at the competitors' lack of consideration. Personally, when I am competing, I find that I am in a far better frame of mind at the start of the day and prefer to work as early as possible. However, there seems to be some magic formula relating success with a late workout.

Another feature of obedience showing which is rather disturbing and may well receive the attention of the Kennel Club Obedience and Working Trials Committee in due course is the unattended dog. Although the owners of 'other breeds' seem to be the main culprits, there is an increasing number of dogs being tied up by their owners whilst they natter, eat or drink. Many of these dogs are becoming very objectionable: the owners do not seem to be concerned about their responsibilities and create socially unacceptable situations.

Although these problems are caused by a minority of

competitors they do tend to create a certain amount of unpleasantness, especially at indoor shows. The main culprits may not be Alsatianists but any good example set by our breed can only help to counteract the declining standards of this minority.

Competitors can make or break a show. Consideration may not keep a venue but the lack of it will certainly be the major factor in losing one.

Appendix 1

Kennel Club Working Trials
Regulations (S1)

(1st January, 1977)

(Reproduced by kind permission of the Kennel Club)

1.   Management of Working Trials – The management of a Working Trial shall be entrusted to a Working Trial Manager who shall be responsible for ensuring that the regulations are observed but he may not interfere with the Judges' decisions which shall be final.

The Working Trial Manager shall be appointed by the Committee of the Society holding the Trial who shall decide upon any matter not related to judging and not provided for in the Kennel Club Rules and Regulations for Working Trials and Obedience Classes and may call upon the Judge or Judges to assist with the decision which shall be final. The Working Trial Manager may not compete at the Trial and should be present throughout.

2.   Judges – When a Judge, from ill-health or any other unexpected cause, is prevented from attending or finishing a meeting, the Working Trial Manager once the Trial has commenced shall have the power of deciding what action is to be taken.

3.   Schedule – A Society holding a Working Trial must issue a schedule which is to be treated as a contract between the Society and the public and neither party is permitted to make any modification before the date of the Trial, except by permission of the Kennel Club, such alterations to be advertised in suitable publications where possible.

The schedule must contain:-
   (a)   The date and place of the Working Trial.
   (b)   The latest date for applying for entry at the Trial. A separate official entry form which must be an exact copy of the wording of the specimen entry form issued by the Kennel Club.
   (c)   The amounts of entry fees and any prize money.
   (d)   The conditions of the draw for the order of running.

(e) The conditions and qualifications for making entries and for intimating acceptance or refusal of entries.

(f) An announcement that the Working Trial is held under Kennel Club Working Trial Rules and Regulations with such exceptions and conditions as the Committee of the Society may decide. Such exceptions and conditions must have received the approval of the General Committee of the Kennel Club prior to publication of the schedule.

(g) The definition of each Stake, together with the qualification or limitations for entry in that Stake.

(h) The names of Judges. An announcement that if the entries in the Companion Dog Stake exceed 30, a Judge may be appointed to judge the Elementary Search and the competitors notified accordingly.

4. Assessing Weather Conditions – The Working Trial Manager and the Judges should assess the weather conditions and should they consider the weather unfit for holding the Trials the commencement may be postponed until such time as is considered necessary for the Trials to be abandoned and the entry fees returned.

5. Handling of Dogs by Owner or his Deputy – An owner or handler may handle the dog, but it must be one or the other; and once the dogs have commenced work an owner must not interfere with his dog if he has deputed another person to handle it.

6. Certification by Judge(s) – The Judge(s) shall certify on a form provided by the Kennel Club that in their opinion the Stake was held in accordance with the Schedule and Kennel Club Rules and Regulations.

7. Disqualification of Dogs – A dog shall be disqualified by the Judges and removed from the ground if in their opinion it is:

(a) Unfit to compete by reason of sexual causes.

(b) Suffering from any infectious or contagious disease.

(c) Interfering with the safety or chance of winning of an opponent.

(d) Of such temperament or is so much out of hand as to be a danger to the safety of any person or other animal.

(e) Likely to cause cruelty to the dog if it continues in the Trial.

If a dog competes which has been exposed to the risk of any contagious or infectious disease during the period of six weeks prior to the Working Trial and/or if any dog shall be proved to be suffering at a Working Trial from any contagious or infectious disease, the owner thereof shall be liable to be dealt with under Rule 9 of the Kennel Club Rules for Working Trials and Obedience Classes.

8. Certificates – The Judge or Judges shall give certificates at a Championship Working Trial P.D. (Police Dog), T.D. (Tracking Dog), W.D. (Working Dog), U.D. (Utility Dog), and C.D. (Companion Dog) Stake to those dogs which have obtained 70% or more marks in each group of exercises in the Stake entered (provided that the dog has complied with any

additional requirements for that Stake). The added qualification "Excellent" shall be awarded should the dog also obtain 80% or more marks of the total for the Stake.

Societies may issue these Qualification Certificates in Championship Stakes to their own design, subject to the approval of the Kennel Club but they must contain the name and breed of the dog, the name of the owner, the title of the Society and date of the Trials, the qualifications and marks awarded and the signatures of the Judge and Working Trial Manager.

The Judge or Judges at Open Working Trials run to these schedules shall give Certificates of Merit for those dogs whose marks would have gained them a qualification "Excellent" at a Championship Working Trial, provided that the Certificate contains the following words: "This Certificate does not entitle the dog named thereon to any qualification recognised by the Kennel Club except entry in appropriate Stakes at Championship Working Trials". Such Certificates of Merit must contain the name and breed of the dog, the name of the owner, the title of the Society and date of the Trial, the Stake and the marks awarded (without reference to any qualification) and the signatures of the Judge(s) and Working Trial Manager.

9.   Prizes – The winner of the Stakes shall be the dog that has qualified with 70% or more marks in each group of the Stake and has obtained most marks. No dog that has not so qualified shall be placed in the prize list above a qualified dog. If no dog has qualified the dog with the highest number of marks may be awarded the prize. Judges are also empowered and instructed to withhold any prize or prizes if in their opinion the dogs competing do not show sufficient merit. Nothing in this Regulation shall apply to the award of "Special" prizes.

10.   Penalties for impugning the decisions of the Judges – If anyone taking part in the Trials openly impugns the decision of the Judge or Judges, he is liable to be dealt with by the Committee under Rules 9 or 10 of the Kennel Club Rules for Working Trials and Obedience Classes.

11.   Order of Running – The order of running tracks shall be determined by a draw and competitors notified accordingly prior to the day of the Trial.

12.   Disqualification for Absence – The Working Trial Manager shall announce the specific time at which a dog or group of dogs may be called for any exercise or group of exercises. Each dog must be brought up at its proper time and in its proper turn without delay. If occasion demands the times and order may be changed at the discretion of the Working Trial Manager with the approval of the Judge or Judges, provided that no hardship is thereby caused to any competitor. If absent when called, the dog shall be liable to be disqualified by the Judge or Judges.

13.   Method of Working – The Judge or Judges in consultation with the Working Trial Manager may arrange for dogs to be working singly or together in any numbers. All dogs entered in a Stake shall be tested as far as possible under similar conditions.

14.   Regulations Regarding Handling.

(a)   A person handling a dog may speak, whistle or work it by hand signals as he wishes, but he can be called to order by the Judge or Judges for making unnecessary noise, and if he persists in doing so the Judge or Judges can disqualify the dog.

(b)   No person shall carry out punitive correction or harsh handling of a dog.

15.   Awards – All awards by the Judge or Judges at a Working Trial shall be in accordance with the agreed scale of points approved by the General Committee of the Kennel Club. Equal awards for any of the prizes offered at a Working Trial are prohibited.

16.   Notification of Awards – The Secretary of a Working Trial shall send (within 7 days of the Trial) the Judges' certification and two marked catalogues to the Kennel Club indicating the prize winners and those dogs to which the Judges have awarded Certificates.

17.   Entry Forms – Entry Forms must be in accordance with the approved form which must be issued by the Secretary of the Working Trial, and all entries must be made thereon and not otherwise, and entirely in ink; only one person shall enter on one form. All such entry forms must be preserved by the Committee of a Working Trial meeting for at least twelve months from the last day of the Trial.

18.   Refusal of Entries – The Committee of any Meeting may reserve to themselves the right of refusing any entries on reasonable grounds.

19.   Objections to Dogs – An objection to a dog must be made to the Secretary in writing at any time within twenty-one days of the last day of the meeting upon the objector lodging with the Secretary the sum of £5.00. The deposit may be returned after the General Committee of the Kennel Club has considered the objection. Should any objection be made other than under Regulation 7(a) to 7(e) the dog should be allowed to compete and a full report made to the Kennel Club.

When an objection is lodged the Secretary of the Society must send to the Kennel Club:-

(a)   A copy of the objection.

(b)   The name and address of the objector.

(c)   The name and address of the owner of the dog.

(d)   All relevant evidence.

The objection will then be dealt with by the General Committee of the Kennel Club whose decision shall be final.

No objection shall be invalidated solely on the grounds that it was incorrectly lodged.

If the dog objected to be disqualified, the prize to which it would otherwise have been entitled shall be forfeited, and the dog or dogs next in order of merit shall move up and take the prize or prizes.

No spectator, not being the owner of a dog competing, or his accredited representative has the right to lodge any objection to a dog or to any action taken at the meeting unless he be a member of the Committee of the Society or of the General Committee of the Kennel Club or a Steward. Any objection so lodged will be disregarded.

20. Withdrawal of dogs from Competition – No dog entered for competition and actually at the meeting, may be withdrawn from competition without notice to the Working Trials Manager. No dog shall compulsorily be withdrawn from a Stake by reason of the fact that it has obtained less than 70% of the marks in any one group.

21. Failure to Participate in Any Exercise – Failure to participate in any exercise in a group in any Stake shall result in failure to qualify in that group.

22. The Working Trials and Obedience Committee shall issue an Appendix to the Schedule of Exercises and Points, "Description of Exercises and Guidance for Judges and Competitors at Working Trials", which they may from time to time alter and in respect of which notice shall be given in the Kennel Gazette.

23. Working Trials for Bloodhounds shall be exempt from Working Trial Regulations 8, 9, 14(a), 15 and 21 and the Definitions of Stakes and Schedule of Exercises and Points. Until further notice the schedule of each Bloodhound Working Trial shall be submitted to the Kennel Club for approval before publication, in accordance with the provision of Rule 3 of the Kennel Club Rules for Working Trials and Obedience Classes.

DEFINITIONS OF STAKES

When entering for Championship or Open Working Trials, wins at Members Work Trials will not count.

No dog entered in P.D or T.D. Stakes shall be eligible to enter in any other Stake at the meeting.

All Police dogs shall be considered qualified for entry in W.D. Championship Stakes if they hold the Regional Police Dog qualification "Excellent", provided that such entries are countersigned by the Senior Police Officer I/C when such entries are made. Dogs holding this qualification are not eligible for entry in C.D. or U.D. Open or Championship Stakes, nor in W.D. Open Stakes.

No Working Trial Stake shall be limited to less than 30 dogs. If a limit is imposed on entries in any Stake, it shall be carried out by ballot after the date of closing entries. Championship T.D. or P.D. Stakes shall not be limited by numbers in any way.

OPEN WORKING TRIAL

Companion Dog (C.D.) Stake – For dogs which have not qualified C.D. Ex or U.D. Ex or won three or more first prizes in C.D. or any prize in U.D. Stakes, W.D. Stakes, P.D. or T.D. Stakes at Open or Championship Working Trials.

Utility Dog (U.D.) Stake – For dogs which have not been awarded a Certificate of Merit in U.D., W.D., P.D. or T.D. Stakes.

Working Dog (W.D.) Stake – For dogs which have been awarded a Certificate of Merit in U.D. Stakes but not in W.D., P.D. or T.D. Stakes.

Tracking Dog (T.D.) Stake – For dogs which have been awarded a Certificate of Merit in W.D. Stakes but not in T.D. Stakes.

Police Dog (P.D.) Stake – For dogs which have been awarded a Certificate of Merit in W.D. Stakes.

CHAMPIONSHIP WORKING TRIAL

Companion Dog (C.D.) Stake – For dogs which have not won three or more first prizes in C.D. Stakes or any prize in any other Stake at Championship Working Trials.

Utility Dog (U.D.) Stake – For dogs which have won a Certificate of Merit in an Open U.D. Stake. A dog is not eligible for entry in this Stake if it has been entered in the W.D. Stake on the same day.

Working Dog (W.D.) Stake – For dogs which have qualified U.D. Ex and have won a Certificate of Merit in Open W.D. Stakes.

Tracking Dog (T.D.) Stake – For dogs which have qualified W.D. Ex and have won a Certificate of Merit in Open T.D. Stakes.

Police Dog (P.D.) Stake – For dogs which have qualified W.D. Ex.

MEMBERS WORKING TRIAL

This is restricted to the members of the Society holding the Working Trial and eligibility for Stakes is as for Open Working Trials.

JUDGES AT CHAMPIONSHIP WORKING TRIALS

For C. D. Stake: Must have judged at least two Open Working Trials and have as a handler qualified a dog "Excellent" in a Championship C.D. Stake.

For U.D. Stake: Must have judged U.D. or W.D. Stakes at two Open Trials, have judged C. D. Stake at a Championship Trial and have as a handler qualified a dog "Excellent" in a Championship W. D. Stake.

For W.D. Stake: Must have judged U.D. or W.D. Stakes at two Open Trials, U.D. Stake at a Championship Trial and have as a handler qualified a dog "Excellent" in a Championship W.D. Stake.

For P.D. Stake and T.D. Stake: Must have judged at two Open Trials, W.D. Stake at a Championship Trial and Qualified a dog "Excellent" in the Stake for which he was nominated to judge.

Note: Service and Police judges are eligible to judge U.D. Stake at a Championship Trial provided they have qualified a dog W.D. "Excellent". They must qualify for approval for other Stakes as above, except that those who have judged all parts at Regional or National Police Dog Trials will not have to qualify as a civilian handler.

KENNEL CLUB WORKING TRIAL CHAMPIONSHIPS

(a) The Kennel Club Working Trial Championships at which Police Dog (P.D.) and Tracking Dog (T.D.) Stakes shall be scheduled are held annually.

(b) The responsibility for organising the Championships each year will normally be delegated to a Working Trial Society approved to hold Championship Working Trials, such Society to be selected by the Working Trials and Obedience Committee from applications submitted by Societies. No Society to stage the event two years in succession.

(c) The Secretary of the Kennel Club will unless otherwise specified be the Working Trial Secretary for the event, the Society scheduling the Championships appointing a Trials Manager.

(d) The following shall be the method of selection of judges for the Championships: – Nominated by Working Trials Societies which have been granted Championship Working Trial status for ballotting by Working Trial Council, final selection by the Working Trials and Obedience Committee.

(e) Dogs eligible for entry in the Championships qualify as follows:-

   (i) T.D. Championship: A dog must have been placed 1st in Championship T.D. Stake and qualified "Excellent" in the Stake during the period 1st October–30th September preceding the Championships.

   (ii) P.D. Championship: A dog must have been placed 1st in Championship P.D. Stake and qualified "Excellent" in the Stake during the period 1st October–30th September in the two years preceding the Championships.

   (iii) Dogs which qualify as above in both P.D. and T.D. Championship Stakes are permitted to be entered in either or both Championship Stakes.

   (iv) The Winners of the previous year's Championship Stakes qualify automatically.

   (v) No other dogs are eligible for entry in the Championships except by special permission of the General Committee of the Kennel Club.

(f) The Championships will normally be held during the third weekend in October each year.

(g) The winner of each Stake in the Championships is entitled to the description of Working Trial Champion.

(h) The Working Trial Society selected to hold the Championships is allowed to forego one Open Working Trial during the same year.

SCHEDULE OF EXERCISES AND POINTS.
COMPANION DOG (CD) STAKE

Group I. Control	Marks	Group Total	Minimum Group Qualifyin Mark
1. Heel on Leash	5		
2. Heel Free	10		
3. Recall to Handler	5		
4. Sending the dog away	10	30	21
Group II. Stays			
5. Sit (2 Minutes)	10		
6. Down (10 Minutes)	10	20	14
Group III. Agility			
7. Scale (3) Stay (2) Recall (5)	10		
8. Clear Jump	5		
9. Long Jump	5	20	14
Group IV. Retrieving and Nose			
10. Retrieve a dumb-bell	10		
11. Elementary Search	20	30	21
Totals	100	100	70

UTILITY DOG (UD) STAKE

Group I. Control	Marks	Group Total	Minimum Group Qualifyin Mark
1. Heel Free	5		
2. Sending the dog away	10		
3. Retrieve a dumb-bell	5		
4. Down (10 Minutes)	10		
5. Steadiness to gunshot	5	35	25
Group II. Agility			
6. Scale (3) Stay (2) Recall (5)	10		
7. Clear Jump	5		
8. Long Jump	5	20	14

Group III.   Nosework

	Marks	Group Total	Minimum Group Qualifying Mark
9. Search	35		
10. Track (95) Article (15)	110	145	102
Totals	200	200	141

WORKING DOG (WD) STAKE

Group I. Control	Marks	Group Total	Minimum Group Qualifying Mark
1. Heel Free	5		
2. Sending the dog away	10		
3. Retrieve a dumb-bell	5		
4. Down (10 Minutes)	10		
5. Steadiness to Gunshot	5	35	25
Group II. Agility			
6. Scale (3) Stay (2) Recall (5)	10		
7. Clear Jump	5		
8. Long Jump	5	20	14
Group III. Nosework			
9. Search	35		
10. Track (90) Articles (10 + 10 = 20)	110	145	102
Totals	200	200	141

TRACKING DOG (TD) STAKE

Group I. Control	Marks	Group Total	Minimum Group Qualifying Mark
1. Heel Free	5		
2. Sendaway and Directional Control	10		
3. Speak on Command	5		
4. Down (10 Minutes)	10		
5. Steadiness to Gunshot	5	35	25
Group II. Agility			
6. Scale (3) Stay (2) Recall (5)	10		
7. Clear Jump	5		
8. Long Jump	5	20	14

Group III.   Nosework

	Marks		
9. Search	35		
10. Track (100) Articles (10 + 10 + 10 = 30)	130	165	116
Totals	220	220	155

POLICE DOG (PD) STAKE

	Marks	Group Total	Minimum Group Qualifying Mark
Group I. Control			
1. Heel Free	5		
2. Sendaway and Directional Control	10		
3. Speak on Command	5		
4. Down (10 Minutes)	10		
5. Steadiness to Gunshot	5	35	25
Group II. Agility			
6. Scale (3) Stay (2) Recall (5)	10		
7. Clear Jump	5		
8. Long Jump	5	20	14
Group III. Nosework			
9. Search	35		
10. Track (60) Articles (10 + 10 = 20)	80	115	80
Group IV. Patrol			
11. Quartering the Ground	45		
12. Test of Courage	20		
13. Search and Escort	25		
14a. Recall from Criminal	30		
14b. Pursuit and Detention of Criminal	30	150	105
Totals	320	320	224

DESCRIPTION OF EXERCISES AND GUIDANCE FOR JUDGES AND COMPETITORS AT WORKING TRIALS

A.   Method of Handling – Although implicit obedience to all orders is necessary, dogs and handlers must operate in as free and natural a manner as possible. Excessive formalism may be penalised, particularly if, in the opinion of the Judge, it detracts from the ability of the dog to exercise its senses in relation to all that is happening in the vicinity. Persistent barking, whining etc. in any exercise other than location of articles, person or speak

179

on command should be penalised. Food may not be given to the dog by the handler whilst being tested.

B.   Heel Work – The Judge should test the ability of the dog to keep his shoulder reasonably close to the left knee of the handler who should walk smartly in his natural manner at normal, fast and slow paces through turns and among and around persons and obstacles. The halt, with the dog sitting to heel and a 'figure of eight' may be included at any stage.

Any act, signal or command or jerking of the leash which in the opinion of the Judge has given the dog unfair assistance shall be penalised.

C.   Sit (2 Minutes) – Dogs may be tested individually or in a group or groups. The Judge or Steward will give the command 'last command' and handlers should then instantly give their final commands to the dogs. Any further commands or signals to the dogs will be penalised. Handlers will then be instructed to leave their dogs and proceed to positions indicated by the Judge or Steward until ordered to return to them. Where possible, such positions should be out of sight of the dogs but bearing in mind the short duration of the exercise this may not be practical. Dogs must remain in the sit position throughout the test until the Judge or Steward indicates that the test has finished. Minor movements must be penalised. The Judge may use his discretion should interference by another dog cause the dog to move.

D.   Down (10 Minutes) – Handlers must be out of sight of the dogs who may be tested individually or in a group or groups. The Judge or Steward will give the command 'last command' and handlers should then instantly give their final commands to their dogs. Any further commands or signals to the dogs will be penalised. Handlers will then be instructed to leave their dogs and proceed to positions indicated by the Judge or Steward until ordered to return to them. Dogs must remain in the 'Down' position throughout the test until the Judge or Steward indicates that the Test has finished. No dog will be awarded any marks that sits, stands or crawls more than its approximate body length in any direction. Minor movements must be penalised. The Judge may use his discretion should interference by another dog cause a dog to move. The Judge may test the dogs by using distractions but may not call it by name.

E.   Recall to Handler – The dog should be recalled from the "Down" or "Sit" position. The handler being a reasonable distance from the dog at the discretion of the Judge. The dog should return at a smart pace and sit in front of the handler, afterwards going smartly to heel on command or signal. Handler to await command of the Judge or Steward.

F.   Retrieve a Dumb-Bell – The dog should not move forward to retrieve nor deliver to hand on return until ordered by the handler on the Judge or Stewards' instructions. The Retrieve should be executed at a smart pace without mouthing or playing with the object. After delivery the handler will send his dog to heel on the instructions of the Judge or Steward.

G.   Send Away and Directional Control – The minimum distance that

180

the Judge shall set for the Send Away shall be 20 yards for the CD Stake and 50 yards for all other Stakes. The TD and PD Stakes shall also include a redirection of a minimum of 50 yards. When the dog has reached the designated point or the Judge is satisfied that after a reasonable time the handler cannot improve the position of the dog by any further commands the dog should be stopped in either the stand, sit or down position at the discretion of the handler. At this point in the TD or PD Stakes the Judge or Steward shall instruct the handler to redirect his dog. In all Stakes, whilst the Judge should take into account the number of commands used during the exercise, importance should be placed upon the handler's ability to direct his dog to the place indicated.

H.   Steadiness to Gunshot – The most appropriate occasion of testing this exercise would be in open country. The dog may be either walking at heel free or be away from the handler who must be permitted to remain within controlling distance whilst the gun is fired. Any sign of fear, aggressiveness or barking must be penalised. This test shall not be carried out without prior warning, or incorporated in any other test. The Judge will not provoke excitement by excessive display of the gun, nor shall the gun be pointed at the dog.

I.   Speak on Command – The Judge will control the position of the handler in relation to the dog and may require the handler to work the dog walking at heel. If the dog is not required to walk at heel, the handler may at his discretion place the dog in the stand, sit or down. The dog will be ordered to speak and cease speaking on command of the Judge or Steward who may then instruct the handler to make the dog speak again. Speaking should be sustained by the dog whilst required with the minimum of commands and/or signals. Continuous and/or excessive incitements to speak shall be severely penalised. This test should not be incorporated with any other test.

J.   Agility – No part of the scale or clear or long jump equipment to be traversed by a dog shall be less than three feet wide nor be in any way injurious to the dog. The tests shall be followed in a sequence agreed by the Judge and will commence with the Scale. The Scale should be a vertical wall of wooden planks and may have affixed on both sides three slats evenly distributed in the top half of the jump. The top surface of the Scale may be lightly padded. The handler should approach the Scale at a walking pace and halt four to nine feet in front of it and in his own time order the dog to scale. On reaching the other side the dog should be ordered to stay in the stand, sit or down position, the handler having previously nominated such a position to the Judge. The Judge should ensure that the dog will stay steady and may indicate to the handler where he should stand in relation to his dog and the Scale before ordering the dog to be recalled over the Scale. A dog which fails to go over the Scale at the second attempt shall be excluded from the stay and recall over the Scale. Failure in the recall over the Scale does not disqualify from marks previously gained.

The handler may either approach the clear and long jumps with the dog or send it forward or stand by the jumps and call the dog up to jump. At no time should the handler proceed beyond any part of the jumps before they have been traversed by the dog. Once the dog has cleared the obstacle he should remain on the other side under control until joined by the handler. The clear jump should be so constructed that it will be obvious if the dog has exerted more than slight pressure upon it. The rigid top bar may be fixed or rest in cups and the space below may be filled in but the filling should not project above the bottom of the top bar. Appreciable pressure exerted by the dog on the clear jump shall be considered to be a failure. Casual fouling with fore or hind legs will be penalised at the discretion of the Judge. Failure or refusal at any of the three types of jump may be followed by a second attempt and any one such failure shall be penalised by at least 50% of the marks allotted to that part of the exercise in which the dog is given a second attempt.

Jumping heights and lengths:-

COMPANION DOG (CD) STAKE AND UTILITY DOG (UD) STAKE

(a) Scale

Dogs not exceeding 10 in. at shoulder	3 ft.
Dogs not exceeding 15 in. at shoulder	4 ft.
Dogs exceeding 15 in. at shoulder	6 ft.

(b) Clear Jump

Dogs not exceeding 10 in. at shoulder	1 ft. 6 in.
Dogs not exceeding 15 in. at shoulder	2 ft.
Dogs exceeding 15 in. at shoulder	3 ft.

(c) Long Jump

Dogs not exceeding 10 in. at shoulder	4 ft.
Dogs not exceeding 15 in. at shoulder	6 ft.
Dogs exceeding 15 in. at shoulder	9 ft.

WORKING DOG (WD) STAKE, TRACKING DOG (TD) STAKE AND POLICE DOG (PD) STAKE

(a) Scale	6 ft.
(b) Clear Jump	3 ft.
(c) Long jump	9 ft.

K. Search - The Companion Dog (C.D.) Stake Search shall contain three articles and all other Stakes shall contain four articles. In all Stakes fresh articles must be placed for each dog who must recover a minimum of two articles to qualify. As a guide the articles should be similar in size to a six inch nail or a match box, but the Judge should choose articles in relation to the nature of the ground and the Stake which he is judging. The time allotted shall be four minutes in the C.D. Stake and five minutes in all other Stakes. The articles should be well handled and placed by a Steward who shall foil the ground by walking in varying directions over the area. Each competitor shall have a separate piece of land.

The C.D. Stake search area shall be 15 yards square, all other Stakes being 25 yards square and shall be clearly defined by a marker peg at each corner.

The handler may work his dog from any position outside the area, provided that he does not enter it.

In the C.D. Stake a maximum five marks should be allotted for each article and a maximum five marks for style and control. In all other Stakes a maximum seven marks should be allotted for each article and a maximum seven marks for style and control.

L.   Track – The track should be plotted on the ground to be used for the nosework by Stewards previous to the day of commencement of the Trials. An area of ground which has had a track laid over it must not have another track laid over it until the following day. The track shall be single line and may include turns. The articles should be in keeping with the nature of the ground. There shall be a marker left by the track layer to indicate the start of the track. In the UD Stake a second marker should be left not more than 30 yards from the start to indicate the direction of the first leg.

Unless the Judge considers the dog to have lost the track beyond recovery or has run out of the time allotted for the completion of the track a handler may recast his dog at his discretion. The Judge should not at any time indicate to the handler where he should recast his dog except in exceptional circumstances.

The track shall be approximately half a mile long and should be laid as far as possible by a stranger to the dog. The article(s) should be well scented. When the judging is in progress the track layer shall be present at the side of the Judge to indicate the exact line of the track and the position of the articles.

The U.D. Stake track shall be not less than half an hour old and shall include one article at the end, recovery of the article not being a requirement for qualification.

The W.D. and P.D. Stake tracks shall be not less than one and a half hours old and shall include two articles one of which must be recovered to qualify.

The T.D. Stake track shall be not less than three hours old and shall include three articles two of which must be recovered to qualify.

In all Stakes the last article shall indicate the end of the track. No two articles should be laid together.

A spare track additional to requirements should be laid but the opportunity to run a new track should be given only in exceptional circumstances.

The area used for Tracking is out of bounds to all competitors for practice Tracks and exercise from the time of the first track and any competitor found contravening this instruction is liable to be disqualified by the Judge and/or Stewards from participating in the Trial in accordance with the provision of Regulation No. 7(c).

The dog must be worked on a harness and tracking line.

M.   Quartering the Ground – The missing person or criminal should be protected to the minimum extent consistent with safety. He should remain motionless out of sight of the handler, but should be accessible on investigation to a dog which has winded him.

The Judge should satisfy himself that the dog has found the person and has given warning spontaneously and emphatically without being directed by the handler. Once the person has been detected and the dog has given voice, he may offer meat or other food which should be refused by the dog. If the dog ignores the food he may throw it on the ground in front of the dog. A dog which bites the person or criminal must be severely penalised.

N.   Test of Courage – This is a test of courage rather than of control. Dogs will not be heavily penalised in this test for lack of control. Handlers must be prepared to have the dog tested when on the lead by an unprotected Judge or Steward, and/or when off the lead by a protected Steward. The method of testing will be at the discretion of the Judge.

O.   Search and Escort – The criminal will be searched by the handler with the dog off the lead at the sit, stand or down. The Judge will assess whether the dog is well placed tactically and ready to defend if called to do so.

The handler will then be told to escort the prisoner(s) at least 30 yards in a certain direction, he will give at least one turn on the direction of the Judge. During the exercise the criminal will turn and attempt to overcome the handler. The dog may defend spontaneously or on command and must release the criminal at once both when he stands still or when the handler calls him off. The handler should be questioned as to his tactics in positioning the dog in both search and escort.

P.   Recall from Criminal. (Exercise 14(a)) – The criminal, protected to the minimum extent consistent with safety, will be introduced to the handler whose dog will be free at heel. After an unheated conversation the criminal will run away. At a reasonable distance the handler will be ordered to send his dog. When the dog is approximately halfway between handler and the criminal he will be ordered to be recalled. The recall may be by whistle or voice. The criminal should continue running until the dog returns or closes. If the dog continues to run alongside the criminal the criminal should run a further ten or dozen paces to indicate this.

Q.   Pursuit and Detention of Criminal. (Exercise 14(b)) – The criminal (a different one for choice) and handler should be introduced as above, and the dog sent forward under the same conditions. The criminal must continue to attempt to escape and, if possible, should do so through some exit or in some vehicle once the dog has had a chance to catch up with him. The dog must be regarded as having succeeded if it clearly prevents the criminal from continuing his line of flight, either by holding him by the arm, knocking him over or close circling him till he becomes giddy. If the dog fails to make a convincing attempt to detain the criminal, it shall lose any marks that it may have obtained under exercise 14(a) or alternatively, it shall not be tested on exercise 14 (a) if that follows exercise 14 (b).

Appendix 2

Kennel Club Regulations For Tests For Obedience Classes (S2)

(1st May 1976)

(Reproduced by kind permission of the Kennel Club)

1. Kennel Club Show Regulations shall where applicable and as amended or varied from time to time apply to Obedience Classes as follows:-

Kennel Club Championship Show Regulations } to Championship Obedience Shows.

Kennel Club Licence Show Regulations. } to Licence Obedience Shows.

Kennel Club Regulations for Sanction Shows. } to Sanction Obedience Shows.

2. A Show Society may schedule any or all of the following classes at a show. No variation to any test within a class may be made. "Run-offs" will be judged, one at a time, by normal scheduled tests.

Classes may be placed in any order in the schedule but this order must be followed at the show except that a Society, by publication in the schedule may reserve the right to vary the order of judging when the entry is known.

The maximum number of entries permitted in a Class for one Judge to judge with the exception of Class C where Obedience Certificates are on offer shall be sixty. If this number is exceeded the Class shall be divided by a draw into two equal halves, each to be judged separately. The prizes for each Class shall be the same as that offered for the original Class. No Judge shall judge more than sixty dogs in one day and if a Judge is appointed for two or more Classes the combined total of entries of which exceed sixty, a Reserve Judge shall be called upon to officiate appropriately. Show Societies should ensure that when appointing Judges for Shows sufficient numbers are appointed for the expected entries. The Reserve Judge may enter dogs for competition at the Show and if not called upon to judge may compete.

Where a Class is divided into two halves exhibitors who have entered for that Class shall be notified accordingly of all changes or alterations and no timed stay exercises are to be held earlier than those advertised for the original class.

In Class C where Obedience Certificates are on offer one Judge only may be appointed for each sex. Should the entries exceed sixty the Judge may approve a Steward who should preferably be a currently active Judge previously approved to judge at a Championship Show, not necessarily for Class C, and who is not a competitor at the show, to report to him the behaviour of the dogs in Sits and Downs in order that the judge might assess the performance. In all classes other than Championship Class C, the same procedure may be adopted should it be expedient to the organising Society. In such cases the steward may be an exhibitor at the show, but not a competitor in the class he is stewarding.

3. *(a)* In all the classes the handler may use the dog's name with a command or signal without penalty. Except in the Stay Tests and Distant Control, all tests shall commence and finish with the dog sitting at the handler's side except in Beginners, Novice and Class A Recall Tests when the dog may be left in either the Sit or Down position at the handler's choice.

(b) Food shall not be given to a dog in the ring.

(c) In any test in which judge's articles are used, none of them should be injurious to the dog, and they must be capable of being picked up by any breed entered in that test.

(d) Spayed bitches and castrated dogs are permitted to compete in Obedience Classes.

(e) No bitch in season shall be allowed to compete in Obedience Classes.

(f) In all tests the points must be graduated.

(g) Handlers may use only a slip chain or smooth collar in the ring.

(h) Every handler must wear his ring number prominently displayed when in the ring.

(i) The Show Executive shall appoint a Chief Steward, whose name must be announced in the schedule, who shall be responsible for the control of any running order and for the smooth running of each class, and whose decision in such matters shall be final.

(j) A draw for the order of running in Class C at a Championship Show must be made prior to the Show and exhibitors and judges must be notified of the order of running before the day of the show. Any published order of running must be strictly adhered to. Except for Championship Class C and at Shows where a draw for the running order for all Classes is made. Show Managements must ensure that an adequate number of competitors/dogs are available for judging in the first hour following the scheduled time for commencement of judging of that Class. All competitors must report to the ring scoreboard steward and "book in" within one hour of the scheduled commencement of judging for the Class and those reporting late will be excluded from competition unless they have reported previously to the Chief Steward that they are actually working a dog entered in another Championship Class C or in the Stay Test of any other Class.

In all Scent Tests, dogs should compete in the same order as for previous tests, but the judge may relax the running order where necessary. Scent tests must not be carried out during the main ring work but will take place as a separate test at the judges' discretion.

(k) Judging rings shall not in any circumstances contain less than 900 square feet of clear floor space and shall be not less than 20 feet in width except that for Championship Class C the ring must contain not less than 1,600 square feet.

(l) No person shall carry out punitive correction or harsh handling of a dog at any time whilst within the boundaries of the show.

(m) Judges at Championship Shows
   (1) For Class C at Championship Shows judges must have had at least three years' judging experience and must have judged at twenty Open Obedience Shows at which they must have judged Class C not less than twelve times.
   (2) For all other classes, other than Class C, judges must have had at least two years' judging experience and must have judged at eight Open Obedience Shows.

(n) A judge of Class C at an Open Show must record in the judging book the number of points awarded to each dog with 290 or more points. The Show Secretary will record these in the official marked catalogue.

4. Imperfections in heeling between tests will not be judged but any physical disciplining by the handler in the ring, or any uncontrolled behaviour of the dog, such as snapping, unjustified barking, fouling the ring, or running out of the ring, even between tests, must be penalised by deducting points from the total score and the judge may bar the dog from further competition in that class.

5. *(a)* In all the following Definitions of Classes, First Prize wins in Limited and Sanction Show Obedience Classes will not count for entry in Open and Championship Show Obedience Classes. No dog is eligible to compete in Obedience Classes at Limited and Sanction Shows which has won an Obedience Certificate or obtained any award that counts towards the title of Obedience Champion or the equivalent thereof under the rules of any governing body recognised by the Kennel Club. Obedience Champions are eligible only for Class C at Open and Championship Shows.

(b) A dog must be entered in the lowest class for which it is eligible by definition and may also be entered in the next highest class if desired, with the exception of Championship Class 'C' for which dogs appropriately qualified only may be entered.

BEGINNERS – If owner or handler or dog have won a total of two or more first prizes in the Beginners Class, they may not compete in Beginners. Winners of one first prize in any other Obedience Class are ineligible to compete in this Class.

Handlers will not be penalised for encouragement or extra commands except in the Sit and Down tests. In these tests, at the discretion of the judge, handlers may face their dogs. Judges or stewards must not use the words "last command" except in the Sit and Down tests.

1.	Heel on Lead	15 points
2.	Heel Free	20 points
3.	Recall from sit or down position at handler's choice. Dog	

to be recalled by handler when stationary and facing the dog. Dog to return smartly to handler, sit in front, go to heel – all on command of judge or steward to handler. Distance at discretion of judge. Test commences when handler leaves dog 10 points

4. Retrieve any article. Handlers may use their own article 25 points
5. Sit One Minute, handler in sight 10 points
6. Down Two Minutes, handler in sight 20 points

      TOTAL 100 points

NOVICE – For dogs that have not won two first prizes in Obedience Classes (Beginners Class excepted).

Handlers will not be penalised for encouragement or extra commands except in the Sit and Down tests. In these tests, at the discretion of the judge, handlers may face their dogs. Judges or stewards must not use the words "last command" except in the Sit and Down tests.

1. Temperament Test. To take place immediately before heel on lead. Dog to be on lead in the Stand position. Handler to stand by dog. Judge to approach quietly from the front and to run his hand gently down the dog's back. Judge may talk quietly to dog to reassure it. Any undue resentment, cringing, growling or snapping to be penalised. This is not a stand for examination or stay test. 10 points
2. Heel on Lead 10 points
3. Heel Free 20 points
4. Recall from sit or down position at handler's choice. Dog to be recalled by handler when stationary and facing the dog. Dog to return smartly to handler, sit in front, go to heel – all on command of judge or steward to handler. Distance at discretion of judge. Test commences when handler leaves dog 10 points
5. Retrieve a dumb-bell. Handlers may use their own bells 20 points
6. Sit One Minute, handler in sight 10 points
7. Down Two Minutes, handler in sight 20 points

      TOTAL 100 points

CLASS A – For dogs which have not won four first prizes in Classes A and B in total.

Simultaneous command and signal will be permitted. Extra commands or signals must be penalised.

1. Heel on Lead 15 points
2. Temperament Test. Will take place before Heel Free. Dog to be in the stand position and off lead. Handler to stand beside dog. Condition as for Novice Temperament Test, except that Test will commence with order "last command" and end with order "test finished". Extra commands will be penalised. This is not a stand for examination or stay test 10 points
3. Heel Free 20 points

4. Recall from Sit or Down, position at handler's choice.
    Dog to be recalled to heel by handler, on command of
    judge or steward, whilst handler is walking away from
    dog, both to continue forward until halted. The recall and
    halt points to be the same for each dog and handler. Test
    commences following handler's last command to dog.   15 points
5. Retrieve a Dumb-bell. Handlers may use their own dumb-bells 20 points
6. Sit One Minute, handler in sight   10 points
7. Down Five Minutes, handler out of sight   30 points
8. Scent Discrimination, handler's scent on handler's article.
    The total number of articles shall not exceed ten, all of
    which shall be clearly visible to the dog   30 points
                                              TOTAL   150 points

CLASS B – For dogs which have not won four first prizes in Class B and
Open Class C in total.

One command, by word or signal, except in Test 2. Extra commands or
signals must be penalised.

1. Heel Free. The dog shall be required to walk at heel free
    and shall also be tested at fast and slow pace. Each change
    of pace shall commence from the "halt" position   30 points
2. Send Away, Drop and Recall. On command of judge to
    handler, dog to be sent away in direction indicated by
    judge. After the dog has been dropped, handler will call
    the dog to heel whilst walking where directed by judge
    and both will continue forward. No obstacle to be placed
    in path of dog. Simultaneous command and signal is
    permitted but as soon as the dog leaves the handler the
    arm must be dropped. (N.B. an extra command may be
    simultaneous command and signal, but an extra com-
    mand must be penalised)   40 points
3. Retrieve any one article provided by the Judge but which
    must not be in any manner injurious to the dog (definitely
    excluding food or glass). The article to be picked up
    easily by any breed of dog in that Class and to be clearly
    visible to the dog. A separate similar article to be used for
    each dog. Test commences following Judge or Steward's
    words "last command" to handler   30 points
4. Stand One Minute, handler at least ten paces away from
    and facing away from the dog   10 points
5. Sit Two Minutes, handler out of sight   20 points
6. Down Ten Minutes, handler out of sight   40 points
7. Scent Discrimination. Handler's scent on article pro-
    vided by judge. A separate similar article to be used for
    each dog and the total number of articles shall not exceed
    ten, all of which shall be clearly visible to the dog and
    shall be similar to the article given to the handler. Judges
    must use a separate similar scent decoy or decoys for each

dog. No points will be awarded if the article is given to the dog

30 points

TOTAL   200 points

CLASS C – At Championship Shows: For dogs which have won four first prizes in Class B, have gained 290 marks on no less than three occasions under three different Judges in Open Class C and have been placed not lower than third on one occasion in Open Class C. Dogs which qualified for entry in Championship Class C prior to 1st May 1976 are also eligible.

At Open Shows: For dogs which have won four first prizes in Classes A or B in total.

At Limited and Sanction Shows: Open to all dogs except Obedience Certificate winners and dogs which have obtained any award that counts towards the title of Obedience Champion or the equivalent thereof under the rules of any governing body recognised by the Kennel Club.

One command, by word or signal, except in Test 2 where an extra command may be simultaneous command and signal. Extra commands or signals must be penalised.

1. Heel Work. The dog shall be required to walk at heel free, and also be tested at fast and slow pace. At some time during this test, at the discretion of the judge, the dog shall be required, whilst walking to heel at normal pace, to be left at the Stand, Sit and Down in any order (the order to be the same for each dog) as and when directed by the judge. The handler shall continue forward alone, without hesitation, and continue as directed by the judge until he reaches his dog when both shall continue forward together until halted. Heel work may include left about turns and figure-of-eight at normal and/or slow pace   60 points
2. Send Away, Drop and Recall as in Class B   40 points
3. Retrieve any one article provided by the Judge but which must not be in any manner injurious to the dog (definitely excluding food or glass). The article to be picked up easily by any breed of dog in that Class and to be clearly visible to the dog. A separate similar article to be used for each dog. Test commences following Judge or Steward's "last command" to handler   30 points
4. Distant Control. Dog to Sit, Stand and Down at a marked place not less than ten paces from handler, in any order on command from judge to handler. Six instructions to be given in the same order for each dog. Excessive movement, i.e. more than the length of the dog, in any direction by the dog, having regard to its size, will be penalised. The dog shall start the exercise with its front feet behind a designated point. No penalty for excessive movement in a forward direction shall be imposed until the back legs of the dog pass the designated point   50 points

190

5.	Sit Two Minutes, handler out of sight	20 points
6.	Down Ten Minutes, handler out of sight	50 points
7.	Scent Discrimination. Judge's scent on piece of marked cloth. Neutral and decoy cloths to be provided by the Show Executive. The judge shall not place his cloth in the ring himself, but it shall be placed by a steward. A separate similar piece to be used for each dog and the total number of separate similar pieces of cloth from which the dog shall discriminate shall not exceed ten. If a dog fetches or fouls a wrong article this must be replaced by a fresh article. At open-air shows all scent cloths must be adequately weighted to prevent them being blown about. The method of taking scent shall be at the handler's discretion but shall not require the judge to place his hand on or lean towards the dog. A separate similar piece of cloth approximately 6 in. by 6 in. but not more than 10 in. by 10 in. shall be available to be used for giving each dog the scent. Judges should use a scent decoy or decoys	50 points

TOTAL 300 points

6. The Kennel Club will offer an Obedience Certificate (Dog) and an Obedience Certificate (Bitch) for winners of 1st prizes in Class C Dog and Class C Bitch at a Championship Show, provided that the exhibits do not lose more than 10 points out of 300, and provided also that the classes are open to all breeds.

Judges must also award a Reserve Best of Sex provided that the exhibit has not lost more than 10 points out of 300.

7. The Kennel Club will offer at Crufts Dog Show each year the Kennel Club Obedience Championship – (Dog) and the Kennel Club Obedience Championship – (Bitch). A dog awarded one or more Obedience Certificates during the calendar year preceding Crufts Show shall be entitled to compete.

The Tests for the Championships shall be those required for Class C in these Regulations. If the winning dog or bitch has lost more than 10 points out of 300, the Championship award shall be withheld.

8. As provided in Kennel Club Rule 4(c), the following dogs shall be entitled to be described as Obedience Champions and shall receive a Certificate to that effect from the Kennel Club:-

   (a) The winners of the Kennel Club Obedience Championships.

   (b) A dog awarded three Obedience Certificates under three different judges in accordance with these Regulations.

EXPLANATORY NOTES FOR OBEDIENCE TESTS
(TO BE READ IN CONJUNCTION WITH
REGULATIONS S(2))

In all classes the dog should work in a happy natural manner and prime consideration should be given to judging the dog and handler as a team. The dog may be encouraged and praised except where specifically stated.

Instructions and commands to competitors may be made either by the judge or his steward by delegation.

In all tests the left side of a handler will be regarded as the "working side", unless the handler suffers from a physical disability and has the judge's permission to work the dog on the right-hand side.

To signal the completion of each test the handler will be given the command "test finished".

It is permissible for handlers to practise their dogs before going into the ring provided there is no punitive correction and this is similar to an athlete limbering up before an event.

Time Table of Judging – To assist show executives the following guide timetable is issued:-

Class C	6 dogs per hour
Class B	8 dogs per hour
Class A	12 dogs per hour
Novice	12 dogs per hour
Beginners	12 dogs per hour

The dog should be led into the ring for judging with a collar and lead attached (unless otherwise directed) and should be at the handler's side.

1. Heel on Lead – The dog should be sitting straight at the handler's side. On command the handler should walk briskly forward in a straight line with the dog at heel. The dog should be approximately level with and reasonably close to the handler's leg at all times when the handler is walking. The lead must be slack at all times. On the command "Left Turn" or "Right Turn" the handler should turn smartly at a right angle in the appropriate direction and the dog should keep its position at the handler's side. Unless otherwise directed, at the command "about turn" the handler should turn about smartly on the spot through an angle of 180° to the right and walk in the opposite direction, the dog maintaining its position at the handler's side. On the command "halt" the handler should halt immediately and the dog should sit straight at the handler's side. Throughout this test the handler may not touch the dog or make use of the lead without penalty.

2. Heel Free – This test should be carried out in a similar manner as for Heel on Lead except that the dog must be off the lead throughout the test.

3. Retrieve a Dumb-Bell/Article – At the start of this exercise the dog should be sitting at the handler's side. On command the handler must throw the dumb-bell/article in the direction indicated. The dog should remain at the Sit position until the handler is ordered to send it to retrieve the dumb-bell/article. The dog should move out promptly at a smart pace to collect the dumb-bell/article cleanly. It should return with the dumb-bell/article at a smart pace and sit straight in front of the handler. On command the handler should take the dumb-bell/article from the dog. On further command the dog should be sent to heel. In Classes A, B and C the test commences on the order "last command" to handler.

4. (a) Sit/Stay – The Judge or Steward will direct handlers to positions

in the ring. The command "last command" will be given when all are ready and handlers should then instantly give their final command to the dogs. Any further commands or signals to the dogs after this "last command" will be penalised. Handlers will then be instructed to leave their dogs and walk to positions indicated until ordered to return to them. Dogs should remain at the Sit position throughout the test. This is a group test and all dogs must compete together.

(b)   Stand/Stay – This test should be carried out exactly as for the Sit/Stay, except that dogs will be left in the Stand position throughout the Test. This is a group test and all dogs must compete together.

(c)   Down/Stay – This test should be carried out exactly as for the Sit/Stay, except that dogs will be left in the Down position throughout the Test. This is a group test and all dogs must compete together.

5.   Scent Discrimination – A steward will place the scented article amongst up to a maximum of nine other articles.

In a scent test if a dog brings in a wrong article or physically fouls any article (i.e. mouths it) this article will be replaced.

The dog should at this time be facing away from the articles. On command the handler should bring the dog to a point indicated, give the dog scent and stand upright before sending the dog to find and retrieve the appropriate article. The dog should find the article and complete the test as for the Retrieve test. In all tests, scent articles are to be placed at least 2 feet apart. Limiting the time allowed for this test is at the Judge's discretion.

Class A – Handler's Scent on Handler's Article.

The Judge should reject any articles he considers to be unfit by nature of their size, shape or substance and which in his opinion could have the effect of converting this elementary Scent Test into a Sight Test. In this test at least one other article must be scented by someone other than the handler and the decoy article(s) must be similar for each dog.

Class B – Handler's Scent on Article provided by the Judge.

The article must not be given to the dog. All articles must be separate and similar.

Class C – Judge's Scent on piece of marked cloth. A decoy steward should not handle a cloth for a period longer than the Judge.

Appendix 3

Working Trials Champions from 1960

DOGS

Dog's Name	Year Qual.	Open Stakes Titles	Sire	Dam	Owner	Handler (If different from Owner)
Mountbrowne Vagus	1960	T.D.Ex. P.D.Ex.	Ch. Cito v.d. Meerwacht P.D.Ex.	Southdown Raider	C.C. Surrey	G. Wraight
Quest of Pasha	1960	T.D.Ex. P.D.Ex.	Letton Pasha of Combehill	Glennis Antoisich	J. Comber	
Dunelm Jamie	1961	P.D.Ex.	Not known	Not known	C.C. Lincolnshire	D. Needham
Quest of Ardfern	1962	T.D.Ex. P.D.Ex.	Cresta of Aronbel T.D.Ex. P.D.Ex.	Letton Questionnaire	J. Cree	
Rolph of Friarsdon	1962	T.D.Ex. P.D.Ex.	Czar of Friarsbush	Danae of Helmdon	K. Cheetham	
Cito of Maco	1962	P.D.Ex.	Ch. Cito v.d. Meerwacht P.D.Ex.	Sigrid von Ruhstadt	R. Matchell	
Dianton Taurus	1963	T.D.Ex. P.D.Ex.	Ch. Bruce of Seale	Diana of Kempton	W. Chadwick	

Pressburg Zorro	1963	T.D.Ex. P.D.Ex.	Ex von Bronning-hausen	Bowesmoor Xyxa	C.C. Surrey	J. Duff
Vikkas Saracen av Hvitsand	1964	P.D.Ex.	Cent zu den Funf Giebeln	Vikkas Glenda av Hvitsand	C.C. Lincolnshire	C. Ogley
Farnrae Rusty	1965	T.D.Ex. P.D.Ex.	Jip (Unr)	Shula (Unr)	Royal Aircraft Establishment	W. Reid
Vikkas Niall av Hvitsand	1965	P.D.Ex.	Vikkas Rando av Hvitsand	Vikkas Tania Super-ior av Hvitsand	C.C. Lincolnshire	W. Darley
Mountbrowne Wotan	1966	T.D.Ex. P.D.Ex.	Ex von Bronning-hausen	Mountbrowne Freya	C.C. Nottingham	J. Rebaudi
Mountbrowne Ajax	1967	T.D.Ex. P.D.Ex.	W.T.Ch. Mount-browne Vagus T.D.Ex. P.D.Ex.	Mountbrowne Netta	C.C. Southampton City	J. Holloway
Mountbrowne Doron	1967	T.D.Ex. P.D.Ex.	Drummer Boy of Drumcot T.D.Ex.	Pressburg Greta	C.C. Surrey	S. C. Wood
Jacopo of Aycliffe	1967	P.D.Ex.	Alf vom Haus Happel	Ilse vom Abtshof	C.C. N.R. Yorks.	F. Taylor
Hero of Hastehill	1968	T.D.Ex. P.D.Ex.	Roon v.d. Sieben Faulen	Ballerina of Hastehill	P. Ostick	
Mountbrowne Huntz	1968	T.D.Ex. P.D.Ex.	Drummer Boy of Drumcot T.D.Ex.	Pressburg Greta	C.C. Surrey	J. Benstead

Dog's Name	Year	Open Stakes Qual. Title	Sire	Dam	Owner	Handler (If different from Owner)
Glenroyal of Callendar	1968	P.D.Ex.	Overend Espresso	Clarendown Alwyn	C.C. Staffordshire	R. Jones
Victor of Aycliffe	1969	T.D.Ex. P.D.Ex.	W.T.Ch. Jacopo of Aycliffe T.D.Ex. P.D.Ex.	Assi v.d. Rheingegend	C.C. Dundee	J. Dykes
Dirk of Caddam	1969	T.D.Ex. P.D.Ex.	Int. Ch. Gorse-field Granit	Ionia of Shraley-carr	C.C. Glasgow	A. Scrimgeour
Atstan Outlaw	1970	T.D.Ex.	Ch. Atstan Impresario	Jewel of Shraleycarr	B. Hall	
Arkwood of Amberwell	1970	T.D.Ex.	Ch. Atstan Luke	Ardent of Amberwell	Mrs. Y. Fisk	
Barrimilne Saba	1971	T.D.Ex.	Gustav of Jugoland	Mepal Lucky Lassie	C.C. Thames Valley	G. Wraight
Wesmid Bowes-moor Gerald	1971	T.D.Ex. P.D.Ex.	Bowesmoor Rock Tadellos	Charm of Bishopsmarston	C.C. West Midlands	G. Garbett
Invader of Hankley	1971	T.D.Ex. P.D.Ex.	Marcus of Hankley T.D.Ex.	Hankley Sindi of Hindrick	F. C. Bell	
Nicki of Hankley	1973	T.D.Ex. P.D.Ex.	Ch. Atstan Luke	Ob.Ch. & W.T.Ch. Ballerina of Hankley T.D.Ex.	F. C. Bell	
Greyvalley Grock	1973	T.D.Ex. P.D.Ex.	Ch. Atstan Impresario	Lowenbournes Kry-stal of Greyvalley	M. J. Jones	

Bowesmoor Falk	1974	T.D.Ex. P.D.Ex.	Quick vom Engingfeld	Bowesmoor Konya	T. Hadley	
Tanfield Wystan	1974	T.D.Ex. P.D.Ex.	Ilk v.d. Esbacher Klippen Sch.H.1	Goldoak Pandora	C.C. City of London	E. T. Buckle
Bois of Limbrook	1974	T.D.Ex. P.D.Ex.	Wilindrek Gustav of Jugoland	Laila of Limburg	Commissioner for the Metropolitan Police	K. Lake
Tanfield Mill-flash Parro	1975	T.D.Ex. P.D.	Ilk v.d. Esbacher Klippen	Stavens Gitta	B. Hall	
Night Raider of Invajendra	1975	T.D.Ex.	Shane of Invajendra	Abbess of Invajendra	J. Allen	
Lance of Amberwell	1976	T.D.Ex.	Ch. Atstan Luke	Lynda of Amberwell	M. J. Jones	
Taypol Amalga	1976	T.D.Ex. P.D.Ex.	Mancraig of Auchensheen	Tina (Unr)	C.C. Tayside	J. Dykes
Bowesmoor Hugo	1976	T.D.Ex. P.D.Ex.	Bowesmoor Inky	Honsbruck Gault Echo	D. Barwick	
Dalynmar Admiral	1976	T.D.Ex. P.D.Ex.	Perham Wayfarer	Zara of Dalynmar	L. J. Tucker	

BITCHES

Bitch's Name	Year Qual.	Open Stakes Titles	Sire	Dam	Owner	Handler (If different from Owner)
Zenda of Stroan	1963	T.D.Ex.	Ch. Beowulf of Seale	Suzanne of Windfalls	C.C. Lincolnshire	J. Etheridge
Hankley Andromeda	1964	T.D.Ex.	Ch. & Ob.Ch. Danki of Glenvoca	W.T.Ch. & Ob.Ch. Amaryllis of Helmdon T.D.Ex.	Mrs D. Foreman	
Ob.Ch. Ballerina of Hankley	1965	T.D.Ex.	Ch. Hortondale Pointsman	W.T.Ch. & Ob.Ch. Amaryllis of Helmdon T.D.Ex.	Mrs D. Foreman	
Ob.Ch. Halan Jill	1966	T.D.Ex. P.D.Ex.	Ch. Cito v.d. Meerwacht P.D. Ex.	Ginny of Pilchards Cove	H. Allan	
Beedawn Lisa	1971	T.D.Ex.	Falcon of Rockverne	Juma of Snittles	A. Hutchison	
Burnaway Freia	1976	T.D.Ex.	Ilk v.d. Esbacher Klippen Sch. H. 1	Burnaway Chiquita of Creslac	Mrs S. Hardaway	

Appendix 4

Obedience Champions from 1960

DOGS

Dog's Name	Year Qual.	Sire	Dam	Owner
Roy's Choice of Elmtree	1960	Rex Prince of Foresthill	Lassie	W. R. Lord
Orpheus of Combehill	1960	Ch. Cito v.d. Meerwacht P.D.Ex.	Grizel of Combehill	G. Rowland
Black Cloud	1961	Dagger of Swyn	Anniss of Swyn	J. P. Coult
Alex of Janpermax	1961	Ch. & Ob. Ch. Terrie of Glenvoca	Sheperdon Katinka of Janpermaz	Mr & Mrs J. Mazur
Carlo of Perrycroft	1961	Trojan of Corvedell	Corvedell Etherow Elegant	J. T. Hudson
Laurel of Vagorlex	1961	Breuse of Seale	Lalique of Kelowna	G. W. Carpenter
Victor of Balterra	1962	Cuno of Elanbriach	Odette of Combehill	H. Allan
Holmflow Rebel	1962	Letton Dusky Despot	Token of Vosta	F. Smith
Bruno of Mendin	1962	Karl of Mendin	Shand of Perrycroft	J. T. Hudson
Jhettanund Daycoss U.D.Ex.	1963	Cuno of Elanbriach	Jacqueline of Wolverdene	R. Crow

Dog's Name	Year Qual.	Sire	Dam	Owner
Flak of Ardgye C.D.Ex.	1964	Aldo of Monasteryhill	Odette of Combehill	S. Duncan
Ricky Royalist	1964	Carl of Notwen	Playful Sheba	Mr & Mrs R. Edwards
Apollo of Hawkswood	1965	Ch. Quixotic of Huesca	Antoinette of Dawnhill	R. Woodcock
Silvershan of Guildhall	1966	Prince of Glenvoca	Carrig Snow	W. J. Spencer
Cordo of Perrycourt	1966	Letton Cordo of Brittas	Keyra of Shalgar	J. T. Hudson
Bwana of Terony	1967	Ch. Bruno of Seale	Jennifer of Jonquest	A. D. Ashley
Grinstede Ranger	1968	Ch. Vasco of Brinton	Norwulf Kelpie	L. Atkins
Heelaway Bestone U.D.Ex.	1968	Int.Ch. Gorsefield Granit	Ob.Ch. Heelaway Cora of Hankley	C. Wyant
Heelaway Amon	1969	Wickesfield Gordon	Ob. Ch. Caroline of Hankley	Mrs K. Wells
Odin of Kenterra	1969	Monarch of Monarchdale	Ava of Monasteryhill	Mr & Mrs R. Scofield
Iliad of Cremas	1970	Penisky's Samuel of Noblehurst	Cleo of Janpermaz	Mrs. R. Davis
Bandino of Roseavon	1970	Ch. Rossfort Curacao	Bracken of Gipsyville	G. Shuttleworth
Prince of Firecave	1970	Prince (Unr)	Hilda of Sutherland	Mrs A. M. Merry
Shar of Howbar	1971	Flawforth Pegasus of Brinton	Lutzi of Howbar	C. Stephens
Heelaway Unit C.D.Ex.	1971	Zasha of Heidanka	Heelaway Fibs	C. Wyant
Shadowsquad Teal	1972	Billo vom Saynbach Sch. H1	Shadowsquad Sonata	G. Thornally

	1972	Golden Boy of Brunton	Tara Tigress	A. Wilson
Schultz of Valhalla	1972	Golden Boy of Brunton	Tara Tigress	A. Wilson
Prince of Ormesby	1972	Cortez of Framley	Lady	D. McDonough
Rodens Bysantin	1972	Gulliver Doreholm	Janetta of Oldway	P. H. Smith
Sabre Potterspride of Brynbank	1972	Bryndale of Harlow	Coral Queen	Mrs. J. Houston
Craigdallie Politician	1976	Dorvaak Crack O'Dawn	Craigdallie Masquerade of Monarchdale	Mrs S. Potter
Garnaza Stefan	1976	Ch. Vondaun Ulric of Dawnway	Melony Ziguener	M. Farrington
Heelaway Usher C.D.Ex.	1976	Ob.Ch. Heelaway Unit C.D.Ex.	Heelaway Zena	Miss P. Thomson

BITCHES

Bitch's Name	Year Qual.	Sire	Dam	Owner
Greyvalley Franzi	1960	W.T.Ch. Cito of Maco P.D.Ex.	Greyvalley Chloe	Miss B. Pindar
Sea Holly	1960	Vaqueel of Kelowna	Isabelle of Rozavel	Mrs N. Hills
Sheba of Dale	1961	Pan of Minstrel	Geraldine of Putland	Mr & Mrs A. Sowter
Lady of Bruderkern U.D.Ex.	1963	Arno of Glenvoca	Alona of Haydock	Miss P. Core
Caroline of Hankley	1963	Orpheus of Hankley	Southdown Fidelia	C. Wyant

Bitch's Name	Year Qual.	Sire	Dam	Owner
Bright Future T.D.Ex.	1963	Eveley's Grim of Charavigne	Jokenhill Jewel	Mr & Mrs W. Highcock
Aniela of Janpermaz	1963	Ch. & Ob.Ch. Terrie of Glenvoca	Sheperdon Katinka of Janpermaz	R. G. Hill
Turo of Eurony C.D.Ex.	1964	Int. Ch. Ilex of Brittas	Cheyenne of Eurony	K. R. Ward
Valeria of Cremas	1964	Iliad of Tollhurst	Sheila of Newington	Mrs R. Davis
Enjakes Kim	1964	Southdown Nireus	Angelica of Codicote	N. Stephens
W.T.Ch. Hankley Andromeda T.D.Ex.	1965	Ch. & Ob.Ch. Danki of Glenvoca	W.T.Ch. & Ob.Ch. Amaryllis of Helmdon T.D.Ex.	Mrs D. Foreman
W.T.Ch. Ballerina of Hankley T.D.Ex.	1965	Ch. Hortondale Pointsman	W.T.Ch. & Ob.Ch. Amaryllis of Helmdon T.D.Ex.	Mrs D. Foreman
Jill of Broster	1965	Auranger of Bryngoleu	Bonnie of Woodlark	J. Brough
Benhooks Zena	1965	Tregiskey Daylight	Benhooks Vanda	Mrs B. Crumpton
W.T.Ch. Halan Jill T.D.Ex. P.D.Ex.	1966	Ch. Cito v.d. Meerwacht P.D.Ex.	Ginny of Pilchards Cove	H. Allan
Janie of Hawgrove	1967	Quest of Jesvale	Freida of Hawgrove	J. Gonzalez
Trudie of Hythefield	1967	Turpin	Nimba	W. Sivyer
Inge Shah of Westonvale	1968	Shah of Danrose	Piddington Sally	J. Reeves
Blondel of Jakalede	1970	Amego of Jakalede	Vikkas Bellona av Hvitsand	H. Lister

Lowenbournes Krystal of Greyvalley	1970	Lorenz of Charavigne	Lowenbournes Dust up	Mrs B. Hill
Kenbellas Joody	1971	Silver Dollar Prince	Pride of Erin	K. Barley
Kikki av Foss	1971	Kilmore Lad	Sheena Dawn of Brighouse	A. Collins
Kinder Syde Raven	1972	Ch. Rossfort Curacao	Vanella of Brinton	Mrs B. Collins
Ranvic Gerda	1972	Terrie of Brinton	Hankley Aquila	Mrs J. Randall
Greyvalley Honey	1972	Ace High	Ob.Ch. Lowenbournes Krystal of Greyvalley	Mrs B. Hill
Daintree Debutante of Hallomas	1972	Observer of Lexter	Gregrise Gay Garland	Mrs. S. Snook
Moorlen Hope Bruderkern	1972	Int. Ch. Asoka Cherusker	Ob.Ch. Lady of Bruderkern U.D.Ex.	L. Moore
Heelaway Cora of Hankley	1973	Ch. Ludwig of Charavigne	Ob.Ch. & W.T.Ch. Hankley Andromeda T.D.Ex.	C. Wyant
Meiklestane Moondust	1974	Ch. Rossfort Curacao	Meiklestane Heirloom	L. Telford

Appendix 5

Dogs Mentioned in the Text

Pet Name	Registered Name	Sire	Dam	Owner
Bob	Barrimilne Caligari Ambassador U.D.Ex.	Ch. Baron of Baileyhill	Clintonville Melissa	C.C. Essex Handler: C. Ball
Callum	Shadowsquad Callum of Ardfern C.D.Ex. U.D.Ex. W.D.Ex. P.D.Ex.	Billo von Saynbach Sch.H.I	Honeysuckle of Brittas	Mr & Mrs J. Cree
Chuffy	Ardfern Assynt	Wascana Glenroy of Robertly	Spagnum of Brittas C.D.Ex. U.D.Ex.	Mrs A. Warren
Cito	Dunmonaidh Cito U.D.Ex.	Molto von Elbbachtal	Hella von Michelstadter Rathaus	C.C. Tayside Handler: W. Rae
Dornie	Drumgesk Catriona	Ilk v.d. Esbacher Klippen Sch. H.I.	Ardfern Brora	Mrs F. Ball

Fraser	Hausfroeng Fraser	Hausfroeng Duval	Centa v. Holzhauserberg Sch. H.I.	C.C. Essex Handler: C. Ball
Honey	Dunmonaidh Centa of Strathleader	Argus vom Klämmle Sch. H.II.	Yalta vom Michelstadter Rathaus of Dunmonaidh	Mrs C. Fairbairn
Jeza	Dunmonaidh Hebe of Ardfern C.D.Ex. U.D.Ex.	Ch. Peregrine of Dunmonaidh	Hexe of Dunmonaidh	Mr & Mrs J. Cree
Kusa	Dunmonaidh Kesta C.D.Ex. U.D.Ex. W.D.Ex.	Merilun of Dunmonaidh	Beldamer Aronia of Dunmonaidh	Mrs F. McFadyen
Quest	W.T.Ch. Quest of Ardfern C.D.Ex. U.D.Ex. P.D.Ex. T.D.Ex.	Cresta of Aronbel C.D.Ex. U.D.Ex. P.D.Ex. T.D.Ex.	Letton Questionaire	Mr J. Cree
Rowdy	Trident of Terager	W.T.Ch. Quest of Ardfern C.D.Ex. U.D.Ex. P.D.Ex. T.D.Ex.	Rosella of Lancilla	Mr E. L. Franklin
Tanya	Spagnum of Brittas C.D.Ex. U.D.Ex.	Int. Ch. Ilex of Brittas	Quixhilde of Brittas	Mr & Mrs J. Cree
Taurus	Dunmonaidh Tetrarch C.D.Ex. U.D.Ex.	Impuls aus Germany	Otti v. Busecker Schloss Sch.H.I.	Miss Moncreiffe of Moncreiffe
Cover Photograph Sappa	Amberwell Viceroy C.D.Ex.	Verus v.d. Ulmer Felswand	Amberwell Trudi	Mrs J. M. Jones

Index